AMERICA
the STRONG

Conservative Ideas to
Spark the Next Generation

WILLIAM J.
BENNETT
AND JOHN T. E. CRIBB

Tyndale House Publishers, Inc.
Carol Stream, Illinois

Visit Tyndale online at www.tyndale.com.

TYNDALE and Tyndale's quill logo are registered trademarks of Tyndale House Publishers, Inc.

America the Strong: Conservative Ideas to Spark the Next Generation

Designed by Jacqueline L. Nuñez

"Cumulative Final Rules Published in the Federal Register, 1993–2013" (page 67) was originally published in Clyde Wayne Crews, *Ten Thousand Commandments: An Annual Snapshot of the Federal Regulatory State* (Competitive Enterprise Institute, 2014). Used by permission.

"Total Welfare Spending" (page 84), "Unwed Birth Rate" (page 199), and "Religious Attendance" (page 216) were originally published in the 2014 Index of Culture and Opportunity, edited by Jennifer A. Marshall and Rea S. Hederman Jr. (The Heritage Foundation, 2014). Used by permission.

"Where Does Every Dollar in Spending Go?" (page 94), "U.S. National Debt 1965 to 2014" (page 103), and "Defense Spending As a Share of the Economy" (page 168) were originally published in Romina Boccia, *Federal Spending by the Numbers, 2014: Government Spending Trends in Graphics, Tables, and Key Points (Including 51 Examples of Government Waste)* (The Heritage Foundation, 2014). Used by permission.

"Trends in Public Schooling since 1970" (page 233) appears in Andrew J. Coulson, "Public School Spending. 'Officials vs. Some Critics,'" *Cato at Liberty* (blog), May 22, 2013, http://www.cato.org/blog/public-school-spending-achievement-media-coverage. Used by permission.

Library of Congress Cataloging-in-Publication Data

Bennett, William J. (William John), date.
    America the strong : conservative ideas to spark the next generation / William J. Bennett and John T.E. Cribb.
        pages cm
    Includes bibliographical references.
    ISBN 978-1-4964-0593-7 (hc)
    1. Conservatism—United States—History—21st century. 2. Values—United States—History—21st century. I. Cribb, John T. E. II. Title.
        JC573.2.U6B46 2015
        320.520973—dc23   2015013275

Printed in the United States of America

21   20   19   18   17   16   15
7   6   5   4   3   2   1

CONTENTS

INTRODUCTION

THE PURPOSE OF THIS BOOK IS to explain what conservatism means. It explains basic conservative principles, the reasons conservatives stand for them, and how they apply to challenges our country faces.

We live in a time when many Americans feel uncertain about the future. They worry about jobs and the economy. They worry about whether the next generation will have a standard of living as high as previous ones. Distrust of major political institutions runs deep. There are concerns about whether the country is on the right path, and even if it might be in decline.

Conservative principles speak to these problems. The United States was founded on conservative principles, and they helped America become a great and strong nation. They can help keep it strong for generations to come.

For that to happen, each generation must pass those principles on to the next. Each generation has to offer clear explanations of certain ideas and values to young people as they reach adulthood. That responsibility has much to do with whether the next generation's future is dim or bright.

The idea for this book grew from questions a smart teenager asked her dad, one of the book's coauthors, John Cribb. The questions came during their drives to school while listening to *Bill Bennett's Morning in America*, the conservative talk radio show hosted by this book's other coauthor.

Questions like "Why do terrorists want to kill Americans?" and "What do you think about global warming?" and "Why shouldn't rich people pay all the taxes?"

And this one: "Exactly what is a conservative, anyway?"

They're the kind of questions some bright young people start to ask when they're in high school or college, or perhaps when they start to vote or get their first full-time job. Questions they ask when they begin to realize that events in the news really do affect them, their family, their friends, and their country.

What is a conservative? This book answers that question and more than a hundred others about issues ranging from immigration to illegal drugs. It examines issues from a conservative standpoint and explains why conservative ideas are good for our country.

If you are a young person just beginning to pay attention to current affairs and politics, there are a couple of things you should know. The first is that nearly 40 percent of Americans consider themselves conservative. Nearly 25 percent consider themselves liberal (the opposite of conservative). So conservatives outnumber liberals by a fairly wide margin.[1]

The second thing you should know is that despite their numbers, conservatives sometimes face questions and even sneering remarks about the values they stand for. Portions of the culture tend to depict conservatism as backward and wrongheaded. They may try to convince you that conservatives are mean-spirited, greedy, prejudiced people.

Most of the national "mainstream media" news organizations in the United States have a strong liberal bias. That includes ABC, CBS, NBC, CNN, MSNBC, PBS, and NPR. (Fox News is the major exception.) It also includes influential newspapers like the *New York Times* and the *Washington Post*.

Liberal journalists outnumber conservative journalists in over-whelming numbers. Only 7 percent of journalists identify them-selves as Republicans (a largely conservative political party). Four times as many identify themselves as Democrats (a largely liberal party), and there is little doubt that the 50 percent who say they are "independent" generally lean left.[2] Many reporters claim to be objec-tive, but they slant their news coverage to favor liberal causes and put conservatives in a bad light.[3]

Hollywood, likewise, is a famously liberal place, and many of the television programs and movies it produces have the same bias. They carry messages that belittle the values and attack the institu-tions many Americans respect—messages like sleeping around is fine, religious people are nuts, and businessmen don't care about poor people or the environment.

College campuses may be the most anti-conservative places in the country. Liberal professors dominate most faculties. At many univer-sities, conservative ideas are shouted down or cut off. "Instructors feel free to mock conservatives in the classroom, and administrators pay scant attention when their posters are torn down or their sensibilities offended," writes a rare conservative Ivy League professor.[4]

Liberal politicians routinely paint conservatives as mean-spirited extremists. President Barack Obama, for example, who is probably the most liberal president in history, told Republicans in Congress, "Stop just hating all the time."[5]

In short, several of America's "elite" institutions give out anti-conservative messages, some subtle and some not so subtle. The bear-ers of those messages aren't interested in helping anyone understand conservative principles. They're interested in smearing those prin-ciples and, if you are conservative, then maybe you, too.

One good way to understand what conservatism is really about is to use the acronym FLINT to remember five core concepts: Free enterprise, Limited government, Individual liberty, National defense, and Traditional values. These five principles are a good summary of conservative thought in America today. They represent ideas, institutions, and values that conservatives prize.

The acronym FLINT has several things in common with the stone flint, a hard quartz that produces a spark when struck by steel. This property made it an indispensable part of the flintlock rifle carried by the Minutemen, who were always vigilant and ready to mobilize in the Revolutionary War.

Like the stone, the ideas represented by FLINT are sound and durable. Like the Minutemen, they stand for strength and vigilance in defense of liberty. They've sparked greatness in the American people and can do so again for the next generation.

You can get a good overview of these principles by turning to the next section. Following the overview, you'll find chapters that go into more detail about conservative ideas and related issues using a question-and-answer format.

The questions in this book are good jumping-off points for discussions about political and civic values. These are important discussions for younger Americans to have with parents and older adults. If they don't take place, it will be hard for the rising generation to understand what this country is all about and to take up its civic responsibilities. It will also be hard for young conservatives to defend their ideas.

It's not easy to come up with off-the-cuff explanations when a young person asks a question like, "Was America founded on Christian principles?" Or when a student says, "My teacher told me that the United States is an imperialist country—is that true?" A lot of times, the first reaction is, "Good grief, where to begin?" We hope that conservatives who have the next generation's best interests in mind can use this book to help supply some answers.

There's an old saying that if you're not a liberal when you're twenty-five, you have no heart, and if you're not a conservative by thirty-five, you have no brain. In other words, liberal ideals often appeal to the passions and enthusiasm of youth, but wisdom and experience eventually lead people to become more conservative.

There is some truth to that, but it's also true that many young Americans are conservative by nature and upbringing, at least in some respects. And it's not always easy for them to face the onslaught of cues from the popular culture telling them that being conservative is backward and wrong.

This book provides some armor for their intellect. It supplies, we hope, reinforcement for conservative beliefs and clear rationales for taking a conservative stance. When people have a good understanding of their own beliefs, they feel more confident sticking up for them when challenged. This book can help conservatives make their arguments with candor, intelligence, and good will.

In reading this book, you may realize that you are conservative about some issues and not particularly conservative about others. Or you may come to the conclusion that you are not conservative at all. That's fine. There is lots of room for differing views in this country. You may not agree with conservative viewpoints, but you should at least know what they are.

We hope that in reading and thinking about the principles discussed here, you find much that appeals to common sense. On a personal level, conservative philosophy is rooted in solid, lasting values that can help you live a good life, one that does good for others. On a political and social level, those values can help your community, state, and country be better places.

We also hope this book helps you understand that conservatives are not people who are stuck in the past. Like this country's founders, conservatives have deep respect for the past and what we can learn from it, but they also welcome new ideas that make good sense.

We believe this country's best days are ahead. But we need to refocus on some values and principles that have made it great. As the

Declaration of Independence says, "a decent respect to the opinions of mankind requires" that we restate those principles from time to time. In the hearts and hands of the next generation, they will help our nation thrive.

CONSERVATIVE PRINCIPLES: AN OVERVIEW

IF YOU'RE WONDERING what it means to be a conservative, this chapter is a good place to start. It gives a general overview of modern American conservative thought, as well as a brief description of its opposite, liberalism.

When you're ready for a little more detail, flip through the chapters in the rest of this book. There you'll find issue-by-issue answers to questions about conservative ideas and values.

What is a conservative?

The term *conservative* comes from the Latin word *conservare*, which means to keep safe, maintain, or preserve. Conservatives want to preserve society's best values and wisdom.

The values that conservatives strive to maintain aren't new. Most have been around for a very long time, passed down from generation to generation because they make life worth living. Values like "love your neighbor as yourself" and "honesty is the best policy." Virtues such as self-discipline, generosity, and gratitude. When we forget or neglect these things, individual lives unravel and civilizations can even come apart.

1

When conservatives step back and look at the world, when they study human activity and history, they see a pattern. That pattern is a set of truths that run through all of time—principles about how best to live and treat our fellow human beings.

These principles aren't truths that each person invents for himself or herself. They are universal standards of right and wrong, or "Laws of Nature and of Nature's God," as the founders of the United States put it in the Declaration of Independence. They were in operation before you were born and will be around long after you die.

The Ten Commandments, found in the biblical books of Exodus and Deuteronomy, are some of the greatest and most famous examples of such timeless moral laws. No better code of conduct has ever been written. When people follow principles like "thou shalt not steal" and "thou shalt not bear false witness against thy neighbour," their lives tend to be fulfilling, meaningful, and good. When they break them, bad things generally happen.

Conservatives recognize that enduring moral truths exist, and they are concerned with preserving ways that help us all live up to them. But conservatives don't claim to be morally superior to everyone else. Like everyone else, they are imperfect creatures. They also realize that the world is a complicated place, that applying principles to life requires judgment, and that sometimes there are exceptions to rules. (For example, killing is generally wrong, but sometimes—for example, in war—killing is necessary.)

Conservatives take history seriously. They know there is much to be learned from the long record of human experience. It reveals both the possibilities and limitations of human nature. History contains much inhumanity and misery, yet an honest reading shows that, despite some great blots, the achievement of Western civilization—and the United States in particular—stands high.

None of this means that conservatives revere and want to preserve everything old. Sometimes old ideas, such as ancient prejudices, need to be rejected. Values are worth protecting only if they do good.

Preserving society's best values and wisdom lies at the heart of conservatism. But there's more to it than that, as you'll see throughout this book.

In America, being conservative involves a commitment to the principles upon which this country was founded, ideals found in the Declaration of Independence, the Constitution, the Federalist Papers, and other writings—ideals such as that all people are created equal and that all have the right to think and speak freely. Conservatives believe that these founding principles have made the United States a powerful force for good in the world.

Although there is no neat and tidy list of American conservative beliefs, there are several ideas that conservatives tend to agree with. One handy way to remember those ideas is the acronym FLINT, which corresponds to the five concepts of Free enterprise, Limited government, Individual liberty, National defense, and Traditional values. These five concepts are critical for understanding American conservative thought.

Free Enterprise

Conservatives recognize that free enterprise—or capitalism, as it's also known—is the best system the world has ever seen for creating jobs and good living conditions. It has lifted countless millions of people out of poverty and made their lives better.

The liberty we enjoy is closely connected to free enterprise. At its best, free enterprise makes possible the liberty we have to choose our own paths, to work toward our goals and dreams.

Free enterprise brings the opportunity to obtain property, whether it be a home, a car, or a new pair of shoes. No one is really free without being able to retain the fruits of his or her own labor.

Conservatives recognize the benefits of competition, which is a vital part of free enterprise. Competition between businesses creates better products and services, as well as lower prices. It encourages entrepreneurship and fosters good, hard work. The competition of free enterprise is a major reason businesses are usually more efficient and productive than government.

For all these reasons, the American founders set up this country to be a "commercial republic," as Alexander Hamilton called it. They wanted it to be a place where business flourishes and where freedom and commerce support each other so people can thrive.

Like any human institution, free enterprise brings problems. It can cause excessive materialism and emphasis on money. Wide gaps can open between rich and poor. Competition can bring out the best in people, but sometimes it brings out the worst. Corporations sometimes take advantage of people, both customers and employees alike.

Free enterprise requires some checks on its darker impulses. Sensible laws can help keep business free *and* fair. Even more important is a culture that values integrity and expects business to be conducted honestly.

Despite its drawbacks, the free enterprise system is without equal in giving people the opportunity to earn a good living. It is a cornerstone of our republic, our liberty, and our nation's success.

Limited Government

Conservatives support the principle of limited government. That means government powerful enough to protect people's rights and vigorous enough to help make the country a better place, but not so powerful that it keeps sticking its nose into people's business and stepping on their liberties.

The founders realized that over time governments have a natural tendency to assume greater power and exert more control over people. "Power whether vested in many or a few is ever grasping," Abigail Adams wrote, "and like the grave cries give, give."[1] In framing the Constitution, the founders did their best to set up checks and balances to curb government's power.

Despite their efforts, today's federal government keeps growing, spending, borrowing, taxing, and regulating. It's now so huge and clumsy that it has a hard time governing even itself. Many of its programs don't work very well. Bills passed by Congress are often so long and complex that few if any senators or congressmen read them before they become law. Researchers at the Library of Congress say that tallying the number of federal laws today is "nearly impossible."[2] Meanwhile, federal bureaucracies churn out thousands of regulations per year.

Government spending is out of control. Every year Washington spends more money than it has. As this book went to press in 2015, the federal debt was a staggering $18 trillion and rising—nearly $60,000 for every man, woman and child.[3]

Conservatives believe we should respect the limits the Constitution places on government. The federal government should focus on vital jobs such as defending the country from foreign enemies, protecting basic rights, enforcing laws, ensuring equal opportunities, and helping people who are truly in need. It shouldn't be smothering businesses with regulations and burying the country under a mountain of debt. It shouldn't be taxing so much that it hurts the economy.

Conservatives recognize that state and local governments, being closer to the people they serve, often do a better job at governing than the federal government in Washington, DC. The elected representatives in state and local governments have a better sense of what works in their regions. And being closer means it's easier for citizens to hold those representatives accountable.

It's a mistake to assume that government has a solution for every problem. Government has important work to do, but in the task of helping society remain intact, much work takes place in the families, neighborhoods, churches, temples, schools, and voluntary groups that make communities good, healthy places to live.

Individual Liberty

The Declaration of Independence states that all people are endowed by their Creator with certain unalienable rights, including the right to liberty. Our right to liberty does not come from government. It is a gift from God. Government's job is to protect that right.

If you look back at history, you realize that most people never got to enjoy much freedom. Most of the world's history is one of rule by kings, emperors, dictators, and governments that told people how they must live. That's still true today in many parts of the world. Liberty is a rare and precious thing, and conservatives are mindful that we must never take it for granted.

Liberty doesn't mean being able to do whatever you want without regard for yourself or others. That is licentiousness, a lack of moral restraint. Millennia ago, the Greek philosopher Aristotle pointed out that liberty is no good unless it involves some limits. "Every man should be responsible to others, nor should any one be allowed to do just as he pleases," he wrote, "for where absolute freedom is allowed, there is nothing to restrain the evil which is inherent in every man."[4]

Conservative thought stresses that true liberty comes with responsibilities. It involves seriousness about acting the right way. It means using your freedom to take charge of yourself and your conduct and owning up to it.

Liberty worth having requires virtues like self-restraint, honor, and respect for others. It involves living up to obligations to family members, friends, neighbors, and anyone who may depend on you. It involves thinking not just of self but of the common good as well.

True liberty implies respecting the rights of others and abiding by the law. In a democracy, it also means abiding by the will of the majority while preserving the rights of the minority. When people neglect those duties, liberty disintegrates.

In a self-governing nation like the United States, it's critical that citizens take responsibility for their own decisions and actions. It's also critical for citizens to assume some obligation for the well-being of their community and their country.

When we don't take responsibility for ourselves and our communities, government often assumes it for us. Whenever that happens, we forfeit some of our liberty.

National Defense

Conservatives have tremendous admiration and gratitude for the United States military. Like most Americans, they place more confidence in it than any other national institution.[5]

To be a conservative is to grasp that men and women in the US armed forces are engaged in a noble effort. When citizens enter the military, they enter an organization pledged to defend the lives of others. They live and perhaps die for other people.

We owe our liberty and our existence as a country to the US military. It is the greatest defender of freedom in the world. There have been times when America has made mistakes with its armies, and even committed grave injustices. But overall the world is a much better place because of the American soldier, and it's a much safer place because our military is strong.

Defending the country from foreign attack is arguably the federal government's most important job. No other part of society is capable of taking over that responsibility.

We live in dangerous times. Islamic terrorist groups have declared all-out war against the United States. They take joy in murdering American citizens. Iran and North Korea routinely make threats. Authoritarian regimes in Russia and China have been signaling an alliance.

Maintaining a powerful military is not only the best way to defend ourselves; it's the best way to keep the peace. It's an expensive obligation. But as General Douglas MacArthur once said, "The inescapable price of liberty is an ability to preserve it from destruction."

Conservatives hate war as much as anyone else. They fully understand the costs of war, including the lost and damaged lives. They know that wars often don't go the way the strategists planned. But they also understand that sometimes war is necessary. "War is an ugly thing," the philosopher John Stuart Mill once wrote, "but not the ugliest of things: the decayed and degraded state of moral and patriotic feeling which thinks nothing *worth* a war, is worse."[6]

Traditional Values

Many of the topics covered in this book touch on traditional values. When conservatives stake out a position on an issue, you can count on it often being one that seeks to preserve those values.

For example, conservatives are strong advocates for freedom of religion, not just because they tend to be religious themselves, but because faith is the anchor of morality for most Americans. Most religions make us better people. Conservatives believe that the country is a better place when churches, synagogues, and other houses of worship flourish.

Family is another institution that conservatives strongly support. It has been said that the family is the first and original Department of Health, Education, and Welfare. It's where the first and most important moral training takes place. Marriage is one of society's fundamental institutions. Good marriages make men and women better people, and they make homes the best settings for raising children.

Conservatives expect schools to be parents' allies in character training. Good schools teach about right and wrong. They make sure students learn math and history, but they also help students become honest, hardworking, fair-minded people who love their country.

Patriotism is an example of a traditional value that conservatives promote. Some "sophisticated" people consider it an outdated, distasteful notion, one that can even lead nations to war. American conservatives believe that patriotism—love of country—is a virtue that leads us to improve our homeland and that the United States deserves our love and gratitude (as well as our willingness to criticize it when deserved).

A deeply held value among many conservatives is that abortion is wrong and that society should protect unborn babies, who are among the most vulnerable members of the human community. The Declaration of Independence says that all of us are endowed by our Creator with an unalienable right to life. Most conservatives believe that children in the womb have that right.

Conservatives understand that culture shapes and reflects people's values. Music, art, books, movies, television shows, websites—they all send messages about right and wrong, about acceptable and unacceptable behavior. It makes a big difference whether the culture is sending messages that marriage is a serious and sacred matter and that doing drugs is dangerous and wrong, or whether it sends messages that no one expects marriages to last and that smoking weed is fine. Traditional values have a hard time surviving if the culture is at war with them.

Are conservatives against change?

No, not at all. It's true that conservatives look to the past for guidance. They want to preserve the best values and wisdom handed down through the centuries. But conservatives also look to the future. They are eager to embrace change that makes sense and is in line with good, sound values.

Change is a necessary and inevitable part of life. Where there is no change, there is no vigor. If we never change, we can never make ourselves better.

In many ways, change is a very American ideal. This country is quick to take up what's new, what's young, what's forward looking. Our nation was born out of change. The Great Seal of the United States, which you can see on the back of every dollar bill, carries the words *Novus Ordo Seclorum*. That's Latin (a very old language) for "A New Order of the Ages," signifying that 1776 marked a historic change—a new democratic era.

Conservatives don't reject change, but they are wary of rapid change because they know it can turn out to be change for no good reason or change simply for the sake of change. They disagree with the notion that everything new is good and everything old is bad. And they are suspicious of politicians who promise radical, sweeping changes that will transform the world. Such promises usually end up bringing more problems than solutions.

When it comes to change, conservatives often prefer to take things gradually. That gives time to see which changes are really good and to preserve conventions worth holding on to.

Conservatism is grounded in reality. It seeks to make the world better, but it does so with the understanding that the world is a complex place, and that often people's ideas to improve it don't work out as planned. Better to move forward step by step than lunge for a utopia that may well turn out to be a mirage.

Conservatives like to look at the evidence before them when tackling a problem and ask hard-nosed questions like "Has this approach worked in the past?" and "Has spending that money really been worth the results?" They are practical minded about reforms but also flexible about considering different approaches as circumstances change.

Prudence comes into play here. Prudence is practical wisdom. It's using reason to figure out the best course to take. Ancient Greek philosophers considered prudence to be one of the most important virtues because it allows us to make good decisions in putting other virtues like courage and perseverance into practice.

Prudence helps us look before we leap. It makes us stop and think through long-term consequences instead of dashing toward a goal without considering the risks.

"I wisdom dwell with prudence," the biblical book of Proverbs says.[7] Conservatives welcome change, but they welcome it with prudence.

Do all conservatives see eye-to-eye on all issues?

No. There are millions of conservatives in the United States, so as you can imagine, they represent a range of views. Get any two of them in a room and they'll agree on many issues, but they'll find at least one or two they see differently.

All conservatives share, to some degree, basic positions like support for the free enterprise system, wariness of big government programs, and concern for preserving the ideals enshrined in the Constitution, Declaration of Independence, and other founding documents. But there is much room for variety.

Here are some terms you'll hear applied to conservatives of different stripes:

- **Fiscal conservatives** are concerned with trying to make the federal government more responsible in its spending habits. They favor less government spending, balanced budgets, and trying to reduce debt. They generally oppose higher taxes, though some fiscal conservatives believe tax increases may be necessary to pay off the government's enormous debt.
- **Social conservatives** focus more on social issues—that is, issues that affect the health of society, such as education, crime, and abortion. They are concerned with preserving traditional moral values. They also want to strengthen the institutions that teach these values, like families and churches.
- **Christian conservatives** are Christians who support socially conservative policies. They apply their Christian values to

questions of politics and public policy. You'll sometimes hear this group called the "religious right," though that term may also include religious conservatives who aren't Christians, such as conservative Jews.

- **Traditionalist conservatives** emphasize the role of tradition and custom in guiding humanity. In their view, each generation inherits the accumulated wisdom, experience, and values of previous generations, kept alive in the traditions and customs that are passed down through time. Radical change that sweeps away traditions may harm society's best values.

- **Neoconservatives** have traditionally emphasized using evidence presented by social science to address problems like crime, poverty, and poor education. They also stress the importance of keeping America's military strong and, when necessary, opposing tyranny overseas. *Neo* means "new" in Greek; the original neoconservatives were former liberals who became conservative in the 1960s and 1970s in reaction to several developments, including the "sexual revolution," rising anti-Americanism on the left, and the left's failure to confront communism.

- **Libertarians** ally themselves with conservatives on some principles. They place their main emphasis on individual liberty and private property rights. They don't like the idea of government using its power to restrict people's freedom of choice. Libertarians don't necessarily consider themselves conservative. Many are conservative on fiscal issues and in their dislike of big government but more liberal on social issues. In foreign affairs, libertarians support free trade and generally oppose US troops being deployed overseas.

There is a fair amount of overlap between these different categories. Many people straddle or fall into more than one group. Some people are conservative on some issues and not so conservative on others.

Conservatives sometimes disagree about how to solve specific problems. That's because applying broad principles to real-life issues isn't easy. For example, it's one thing to believe that limited government is a good thing but quite another to decide exactly how much to limit government spending on programs like defense or aid to the poor.

The bottom line is that while conservatives agree on some fundamental principles, there is much diversity of opinion among their ranks. That's a good thing. Variety is often a sign of rich ideas and healthy debate.

How are liberals different from conservatives?

Liberals lie on the opposite side of the range of political opinions from conservatives. You'll sometimes hear them called "progressives" or "the left" (as opposed to "the right" or "the right wing," as conservatives are often called). Liberals are likely to vote for Democratic candidates and conservatives for Republicans, although that rule does not always hold true.

Liberals have much more faith than conservatives in the ability of the government to fix society's problems. They like the idea of the federal government in Washington, DC, running big programs that provide lots of services to people. Generally speaking, they place great confidence in the idea of skilled and knowledgeable government officials managing society at every level.

In essence, liberals want to use the power of government to reengineer society. The dream of many liberals is a government that provides services for everyone at every stage of life (a cradle-to-grave "nanny state," as conservatives often call it).

Liberals generally favor more government spending and higher taxes to fund more government programs. They are not as concerned about the government running up debt in order to fund more programs.

Many liberals are suspicious of the free enterprise system. They see it as a source of much inequality and unfairness in the world. They're often in favor of more government regulation to exert more control over business activities.

In the view of many liberals, one of the chief roles of government is to make things more equal in terms of people's income and material possessions. They support using the tax system to redistribute wealth from people with more to people with less.

Liberals are generally inclined to spend less than conservatives on defense and the military. They would rather spend money on social programs. Some liberals take a skeptical view of the military and regard it as an agent of destruction.

Liberals tend to attribute many of society's problems to racism, gender discrimination, and divisions between rich and poor. They often think of themselves as defenders of minorities and groups that have suffered discrimination in the past, such as blacks, women, and gays.

Extreme liberals (sometimes called "radical leftists") view American history largely in terms of its failures. They look at the American record as one of mistreatment of minorities, exploitation of the poor, and imperialism toward weaker nations.

As you can imagine, conservatives and liberals disagree on many political issues. For example, while conservatives in general believe that abortion is wrong and that society should protect unborn babies, many liberals support abortion rights. Liberals are more inclined than conservatives to believe that climate change is a serious threat and that government should regulate human behavior to slow down global warming. They are more likely than conservatives to believe that government should play a greater role in running the nation's health care system.

It's important to remember that conservatives and liberals are political opponents, but they're not enemies. They're fellow

Americans. Our enemies are those who want to do us harm, like Islamic terrorist organizations.

It's also important to remember that despite their differences, conservatives and liberals share many beliefs. For example, we can all agree on the importance of virtues like honesty, perseverance, and compassion. When conservatives say things like "We should honor our police officers for upholding the law and keeping us safe," the large majority of liberals would say, "I believe that too."

Conservatives and liberals share many of the same goals. They want people to get good educations and good jobs and to be happy and live good lives. They want the United States to be a nation that lives up to its finest promises. But ask a conservative and a liberal how to make all that happen, and you'll often get profound disagreement.

THE AMERICAN
RECORD

NORMAN BORLAUG, a descendent of Norwegian immigrants, grew up in the early part of the twentieth century on an Iowa farm, where a boy couldn't help but learn a thing or two about how corn and wheat grow. He attended a one-room school, worked his way through college during the Great Depression, and then earned a doctorate in plant pathology.

During World War II, when massive destruction raised fears of widespread hunger, he plunged into the work of helping impoverished countries grow more food. He headed to Mexico to join a program funded by the Rockefeller Foundation to help farmers produce more crops.

His initial efforts didn't turn out very well. Borlaug taught the farmers to feed their wheat crops extra nitrogen to increase yields, but the stalks grew so tall and heavy that they collapsed. He tackled the problem by developing shorter, stouter plants that could support abundant wheat grains. For years he battled the tropical sun, floods, disease, and drought as he showed farmers the best way to plant, fertilize, and irrigate.

By the 1960s, when experts were warning that global famine was just a few years away, Mexican farmers were producing enough grain to feed their own people and even export a surplus. It was the beginning of an agricultural revolution that swept much of the world. Pleas for help arrived from other poor countries with starving populations. Dr. Borlaug and his colleagues traveled throughout Asia, Africa, and Latin America to spread their techniques and breed new plants. Grain production soared.

Before he died in 2009, Norman Borlaug received the Nobel Peace Prize, the Presidential Medal of Freedom, the Congressional Gold Medal, and scores of other tributes. By some estimates, his work helped save the lives of one billion people around the world.[1]

His is an extraordinary story, a very American story, because America is the place where, more than any other country, extraordinary efforts are launched and ideas born. In many ways the United States has been, and continues to be, one of the most amazing countries in history.

What's so great about the American record?

If you listen to the cynics and critics, there isn't much to admire about America. Some history books and professors give the impression that this country is fundamentally flawed and unfair and that Americans have much to apologize for: stealing land from Native Americans, fouling the environment, enslaving Africans, withholding rights from women, exploiting laborers, discriminating against people of color, and waging imperialist wars against the third world.

Even Norman Borlaug was denounced by left-wing environmentalists who said his techniques used too many chemicals and caused small farmers in Africa and other parts of the world to be replaced by large-scale, corporate operations. Borlaug responded that if his critics "lived just one month amid the misery of the developing world, as I have for 50 years, they'd be crying out for tractors and fertilizer and irrigation canals and be outraged that fashionable elitists in wealthy nations were trying to deny them these things."[2]

If you take a step back and look at the broad picture, you see just how remarkable the American record is. For example:

- **The United States was the first nation in history created out of the belief that people should govern themselves.** As James Madison said, this country's birth was "a revolution which has no parallel in the annals of human society."[3] The US Constitution is the oldest written national constitution in operation. It has been a model for country after country as democracy has spread across the world.
- **The US military is the greatest defender of freedom in the world.** From the time of the Revolutionary War, Americans have been willing to put themselves in harm's way for freedom. The US military led the way in defeating Fascism during World War II, then led the free world in the decades-long struggle against communism during the Cold War. It continues the fight against Islamic terrorism.

  As General Colin Powell said, "We have gone forth from our shores repeatedly over the last hundred years . . . and put wonderful young men and women at risk, many of whom have lost their lives, and we have asked for nothing except enough ground to bury them in, and otherwise we have returned home . . . to live our own lives in peace."[4]
- **No other country has done a better job of establishing equal rights for all citizens.** Certainly there have been times when the United States has fallen tragically short of its founding principles. But especially in recent decades, no country has worked harder to eliminate discrimination and protect the rights of minorities. There are plenty of nations where people's ethnicity, religion, or gender define them as second-class citizens. In contrast, America has been a pioneer in striving toward the ideal that all people are created equal.

- **No other country has welcomed and united so many people from so many different shores.** Never before have so many people from different backgrounds, races, nationalities, and religions lived and worked together so peacefully. In no other nation has the spirit of brotherhood accomplished more than it has in the United States.

  There is a simple test for a country. It's called the Gates Test. Every country has gates of some kind. When it raises its gates, which way do people run? Do they rush to get in, or do they run to get out? When the United States raises its gates, people rush in.

- **American companies have made the United States one of the most powerful economic engines the world has known and one of the most prosperous countries in history, with one of the world's highest standards of living.** American companies provide some of the best jobs in the world. They've also built innumerable hospitals, libraries, and parks; created great universities; filled museums with works of art; found cures for diseases; and improved human life in countless ways.

- **The United States is the world's greatest marketplace for the free exchange of ideas and information.** In some countries, governments shut down newspapers and broadcast stations they don't like and limit access to the Internet. Freedom of expression and freedom of the press are bedrock principles of American democracy. The staggering volume of information traded here every day—via books, newspapers, magazines, the Internet, TV, and radio—makes this country the liveliest center of thought and debate in history.

- **America is a world leader in scholarship and invention.** It is home to the world's finest collection of universities and research institutions. Name just about any subject—from ancient philosophy to quantum physics—and chances are good that leading authorities work here. The record of American inventions and discoveries goes on and on, from the mechanical reaper to the microchip. American medical research facilities are among the best in the world. The United States leads the world in space exploration. The computer revolution started here.

- **This country is the planet's largest source of humanitarian aid.** When disasters strike overseas, Americans are among the first to offer support. Canadian journalist Gordon Sinclair once called Americans "the most generous and possibly the least-appreciated people in all the world." He said, "When I first started to read newspapers, I read of floods on the Yellow River and the Yangtze. Well, who rushed in with men and money to help? The Americans did, that's who. . . . I can name to you 5,000 times when the Americans raced to the help of other people in trouble. Can you name to me even one time when someone else raced to the Americans in trouble?"[5]

None of this means that Americans are better than everyone else, or that the United States is always right, or that the country is without faults. Of course it has many faults; its history includes wrongs such as slavery, segregation, and the denial of women's rights. All human institutions are imperfect. Yet over the years Americans have shown themselves to be pretty good at taking a hard look at the nation's wrongs and trying to make them right.

The late senator Daniel Patrick Moynihan put it this way: "Am I embarrassed to speak for a less-than-perfect democracy? Not one bit. Find me a better one. Do I suppose there are societies that are free of sin? No, I don't. Do I think ours is on balance incomparably the most hopeful set of human relations the world has? Yes, I do. Have we done obscene things? Yes, we have. How did our people learn about them? They learned about them on television and in the newspapers."[6]

A country, like a person, should be judged by the totality of its acts. In any honest assessment, America's total record stands tall—tall enough to be called great.

What does "American exceptionalism" mean?

American exceptionalism is the idea that the United States has a character and set of ideals that sets it apart from other countries. Those ideals have led it to play a unique role in history, as evidenced by the record outlined above.

The idea of American exceptionalism has been around since European immigrants began coming to these shores. "We must consider that we shall be as a city upon a hill," Puritan leader John Winthrop wrote. "The eyes of all people are upon us."[7]

He was right. For most of this country's history, the world has watched to see how America has struggled to live up to its promise. Sometimes we've fallen short, even tragically short, but often we've attained heights long thought unreachable.

What makes this country truly exceptional are the promises and principles of America—the old truths written into the Declaration of Independence and Constitution. Freedom of thought and speech. Equality before the law. The right to worship God as we please. The dignity of each individual. The freedom to pursue dreams and the opportunity to live to our fullest potential.

Such ideals, perhaps more than anything else, make us who we are. They're the glue that holds the United States together. They're what we stand for.

Many people around the world look to the United States as the standard-bearer of those ideals, especially freedom. Perhaps in the end what makes America exceptional is that often we do finally live up to our ideals. America is that special place where people's dreams about it do indeed come true.

No, not everyone likes America. There will always be detractors and enemies. But for millions overseas, Americans are "the watchmen on the walls of world freedom."[8] Americans are at their best when they stand up for the founding principles and fight for them, when necessary.

Some liberals believe that American exceptionalism is a dangerous myth, the invention of an arrogant country that wants to throw its weight around. Our military is too heavy handed, our carbon footprint too large, our policies too pushy, they say. The world would be better off and like us a lot better if we'd stop acting like we're so exceptional.

Conservatives believe that the answer to those kinds of criticisms is the American record itself. All in all, despite its blemishes, it's an extraordinary record. The world is a better place because of it.

Is patriotism an outdated notion?

There are always people who view patriotism as something slightly embarrassing and unsophisticated, an awkward sentiment out of step with modern times. They think of it as a "down-market commodity," a cheap and easy thing. Such people get nervous that waving the American flag will make people want to start a war or step on other countries. They prefer to think of themselves as citizens of a global community.

These "sophisticated" people are confusing patriotism (love of country) with jingoism (excessive devotion to country, often marked by aggression toward other nations). Love of country is a good thing.

Patriotism doesn't mean obnoxious boasting, but it does involve taking pride in our country's achievements, sticking up for its principles, supporting its efforts, and cheering it on at times. It means offering respect to our nation and to its institutions.

True patriotism is *informed* patriotism. When you really love something, you recognize its strengths and faults. Patriots are what

James Madison called "loving critics" who examine their country's actions closely, raise concerns when necessary, and try to make their nation as good as it can possibly be.

Conservatives aren't shy about critiquing their country, but they're also not shy about celebrating American ideals and all the good this country has done. They certainly aren't the only people to take pride in the United States. But one mark of conservatism is to be unembarrassed to say that this is a great and good nation.

Why is it important to say that?

First, because it is the truth, and the truth is always worth saying. If we forget the truth about this country's greatness, we stop being a great people. We weaken the American spirit.

Second, recognizing America's greatness helps make us grateful. No other country has ever offered so much opportunity to learn, to grow, to make a living, to make a mark. We can't take that for granted. Let us not commit the sin of ingratitude for so many blessings.

Third, recognizing America's goodness helps us love this country. And loving it makes us want to protect it. Nothing good lasts when people don't cherish and protect it. If we don't stand up for America, it will disappear.

One of the best ways to appreciate this country is to learn about its history. Do a little reading about Washington's crossing the Delaware, the building of the transcontinental railroad, the march on Selma, or the landing on the moon. Visit places like Kitty Hawk, the Alamo, or Pikes Peak. The more you know American history, the more you come to realize that it is one of the greatest stories of all time. And you come to see why Abraham Lincoln called the United States the "last best hope of earth."[9]

Part 1

FREE ENTERPRISE

FREE
ENTERPRISE

One summer day in 1807, a crowd gathered on the bank of the Hudson River in New York to watch Robert Fulton launch a "boat driven by a tea kettle." People called it "Fulton's folly" and predicted it would explode. Fulton lit the boiler, and the boat chugged up the river at an astounding four miles per hour. The *Clermont*, the first commercially successful steamboat, marked a new age of steam transportation.

Orville and Wilbur Wright dreamed up the first airplane in their bicycle shop in Dayton, Ohio. They experimented with model wings in a wind tunnel built out of an old washtub, a fan, and a wooden box. One of the nation's leading scientists had shown by "unassailable logic" that human flight was impossible. But on a frigid December morning in 1903 at Kitty Hawk, North Carolina, the Wright brothers' plane lifted into the air with Orville aboard and launched the age of flight.

In the early 1970s, Motorola Corporation began developing a

wireless phone that people could carry around with them. One day in 1973, Motorola engineer Martin Cooper stood on a sidewalk in Manhattan, punched a number into a handset while pedestrians gave him curious looks, and made the first cell phone call. "Joel, I'm calling you from a cellular phone," he told his counterpart at rival Bell Labs, "a real cellular phone, a handheld, portable, real cellular phone."[1] That first cell phone was as large as a brick and weighed two and a half pounds. Within four decades, billions of people worldwide had pocket-sized phones.

On April Fool's Day 1976, twenty-five-year-old computer hobbyist Steve Wozniak ("Woz" to fellow nerds) and his friend Steve Jobs, twenty-one, formed a company to sell a computer circuit board that Wozniak had built. Jobs sold his Volkswagen minibus and Wozniak sold his programmable calculator to fund their efforts. They assembled the circuit boards in the Jobs's garage. It was the beginning of Apple, Inc.

All of those ventures were made possible by a system that in itself is a miracle, one that has transformed the world again and again—free enterprise.

Free enterprise is an economic system in which property, resources, and industry are controlled by individuals and businesses to make profits. Another name for free enterprise is capitalism, although free enterprise is in many ways a more accurate term since the freedom to conduct business is one of its bedrock principles.

Is free enterprise good or bad for the world?

Free enterprise has its drawbacks, but overall it's a terrific economic system—the best the world has known. It's certainly the best system in history for creating jobs and material well-being. Even government jobs depend on it since tax revenues generated by free enterprise pay government workers' salaries.

In free markets, companies have to compete against each other for profits. That competition encourages businesses to offer the best possible products and services for the lowest cost. That puts a higher standard of living within more people's reach. Opportunity unleashes the creativity of inventors and entrepreneurs. That creativity drives civilization forward, from steamboats to airplanes to cell phones.

One way to appreciate free enterprise is to look at what life was like before it came along. Modern free enterprise, or capitalism, began in Great Britain along with the Industrial Revolution in the latter part of the eighteenth century. Before then, cities such as London were filthy, violent places where most people struggled simply to make it from one day to the next.

A child born in London around 1750 faced poor odds—as low as 25 percent—of living past age five.[2] Most people were illiterate. Poverty and disease were rampant. Jobs were hard to come by and often fleeting. The masses owned little more than the clothes on their backs. They had almost no hope that their lives or their children's lives would ever be any better.[3]

In the short term, free enterprise and industrialism did little to improve people's conditions—in some ways, they may have made things worse. You've probably read Charles Dickens's descriptions of early industrial towns full of soot-covered streets and dark factories with chimneys "out of which interminable serpents of smoke trailed themselves for ever and ever, and never got uncoiled."[4]

But over time, as nations and cities adjusted to the upheaval brought on by rapid change, something close to miraculous happened. For millions of people, life got immeasurably better as they gained access to mass-produced goods—clothes, furniture, books, and automobiles. As business increased, so did job opportunities. A middle class emerged. Literacy spread. Incomes rose. People began to live much longer. Free enterprise was not solely responsible for these changes, but it had a great deal to do with them.

If you want to see the stark difference between life with free enterprise and life without it, search the Internet for "North Korea night photo." Take a look at one of the nighttime satellite images of North Korea, a country run by a harsh dictatorship that controls the economy, and neighboring South Korea, a vibrant republic where free enterprise thrives. The darkness of North Korea is a sobering sight.

Yes, there is a troubling side to free enterprise. There are booms and busts. People get laid off, sometimes at the worst of times, as companies watch their bottom lines. In some parts of the world, workers labor in sweatshops.

But overall, the effects of free enterprise have improved people's lives in countless ways. It is difficult to imagine what life would be like without mass-produced electric lights, washers, telephones, medicines, vaccines, motors, pens, soap, tires—the list goes on and on.

As Peter Wehner and Arthur C. Brooks write in their book *Wealth and Justice: The Morality of Democratic Capitalism* (to which this chapter is indebted), "The history of the last three centuries is indisputable: The rewards and benefits of capitalism far outweigh the drawbacks. In our view, it is not really a close call."[5]

Doesn't free enterprise make some people rich while others remain poor?

The median pay package of CEOs at large American companies was over $10 million in 2013.[6] Some of those businesspeople put on lavish displays of wealth with their mansions, yachts, and private jets.

It's enough to make some people ask, "Is that fair, when so many people are struggling? Is it too much money?"

The first point to realize is that free enterprise can't make everyone wealthy. No economic system can. We can't all be rich. It's just a fact of life we need to accept.

But the second point is just as important: while making relatively few people rich, free enterprise brings countless others good incomes. It can help make everyone better off.

A woman who founds and spends twenty years building a biotech company might (or might not) make a lot of money for herself, but along the way her company provides jobs for its employees, jobs that otherwise would not exist. That's a very good thing. In this way, free enterprise has done more to employ people, lift them out of poverty, and improve their lives than any other economic system in history.[7]

"Fine," you might say, "let some people make lots of money, but not *that* much money—not $10 million a year!" The problem with this argument is that it raises the question, Who gets to decide how much money people should make? The government? Should officials in Washington, DC, have the power to decide how much that woman who built the biotech company with twenty years of hard work should make? Is that fair? Should a nameless bureaucrat get to decide how much *you* can make?

If you take away people's chances to earn money and even make themselves rich, you take away much of their incentive to work hard, take risks, and launch new businesses. Do that, and people have much less reason to build companies like Apple, Google, and General Electric—or smaller companies like your local bank and hardware store. Then everyone loses, especially people who need jobs at those companies.

Fans of free enterprise need to acknowledge that huge income gaps between a company's management and its workers can lead to resentment. That can be bad for the company and all involved. It's something corporations must keep in mind.

People who make lots of money should remember, as Saint Paul tells us, that "God loveth a cheerful giver."[8] It's also smart to remember that the Bible warns again and again of the dangers that wealth brings.

As for those among us who don't make lots of money, it's good to remember that free enterprise offers the best opportunity to rise in the world and to make more money, perhaps even creating more jobs for others along the way. As Abraham Lincoln said, "The man who labored for another last year, this year labors for himself, and next year he will hire others to labor for him."[9]

Is free enterprise a moral system?

Critics say that free enterprise causes greed and excessive ambition. It turns life into a vicious competition in which the ruthless and dishonest exploit others to come out ahead.

In truth, sometimes people can and do act immorally in business—just as people sometimes act immorally in government or in their family lives. Human beings are imperfect creatures, and any system involving humans can lead to abuses and corruption. But we must weigh the good against the bad.

Yes, free enterprise is driven largely by self-interest, as the moral philosopher Adam Smith pointed out in his great book *The Wealth of Nations*, published in 1776. People are naturally interested in getting things they need and want for happy, comfortable lives.

But self-interest is not the same as selfishness. We can be interested in improving our own lives while at the same time helping others. That's what most business owners do when they hire people or when they sell products that people want. They are helping others while they help themselves.

In many ways, free enterprise can actually help us become better people because it encourages us to exercise several virtues. In work we learn responsibility and reliability when tasked with projects large and small. We gain perseverance in meeting tough deadlines. We learn about cooperation in dealing with colleagues and about civility in relations with customers, employers, and employees.

Entrepreneurs exercise creativity in coming up with new ideas. They develop habits of thrift in saving to start a business and dedication in getting it off the ground. Managers and employees alike learn the value of honesty because the reality is that in the world of business, dishonesty is one of the surest ways to lose a business or get fired.

That said, the main purpose of free enterprise is to help people prosper and have more comfortable lives, not maintain virtue. To make sure people act morally and treat each other fairly in a free enterprise system, we have to look outside of free enterprise itself.

Government can help here. Laws that keep businesses from putting children to work or dumping chemicals in streams, for example, are good checks on free enterprise. As long as they don't hamper business with too much red tape, legislatures and courts can be business's allies in improving lives.

More important than government, though, is culture. The morality of any society's economic system depends on the morality of its culture. A corrupt culture will produce corrupt enterprise (and corrupt government). A decent culture will produce businesses that treat people well.

That means our most important institutions—families, churches and other houses of worship, neighborhoods, schools, and communities—must help produce people of good character who make good employers and employees. It takes a lot of work to maintain a culture that keeps capitalism within moral bounds. In a world full of commercialism, attention to virtue helps keep money and the things it can buy in perspective.

Calvin Coolidge, the thirtieth president of the United States, is famous for saying that "the chief business of the American people is business." But he also reminded us that for all the prosperity that free enterprise has brought this country, without dedication to some deeper matters, it's all for nothing. "The things of the spirit come first," he said. "Unless we cling to that, all our material prosperity, overwhelming though it may appear, will turn to a barren sceptre in our grasp."[10]

Does socialism work?

Socialism is a political and economic system in which the government controls the means of production (such as factories and land) and the distribution of income. In essence, government control replaces the free markets of capitalism.

Virtually all Western nations, including the United States, have "mixed economies"—that is, economies that contain some elements of socialism mixed with free-market capitalism. The mixture varies from nation to nation. Political debates often involve the question of how far government control over a nation's economy should go.

Some people on the left are attracted to the idea of socialism because it promises more economic equality. Because government has more control over the economy, the theory goes, it can make sure workers receive a greater share of goods.

The real-world record of nations that have veered toward socialism, however, is not good.

One reason socialist countries have often failed is that it's virtually impossible for government officials—or for anyone—to plan and run an economy. Economies are enormously complex, made of countless interacting forces. No one fully understands how they work. Over time, centralized government control doesn't work well.

More important, socialist countries take freedom away from people. Since the government assumes more control, individuals have fewer choices. If you have an idea to start a business and it doesn't fit into the government's plans, too bad for you—you might wait years for a permit to start that business, if it ever comes at all.

Someone once said that the problem with socialism is socialism, while the problem with capitalism is capitalists. Capitalism, despite the good it does, is sometimes abused by people. Socialism, on the other hand, is itself a fundamentally flawed system.

Socialism demoralizes people while making them dependent

on the state. It promises equality but in fact levels everyone down (except the ruling authorities) by taking away liberty. As Pope John Paul II wrote,

> In the place of creative initiative there appears passivity, dependence and submission to the bureaucratic apparatus which, as the only "ordering" and "decision-making" body— if not also the "owner"—of the entire totality of goods and the means of production, puts everyone in a position of almost absolute dependence. . . . This provokes a sense of frustration or desperation and predisposes people to opt out of national life.[11]

Cuba is a nearby socialist nation. A journalist on a recent visit wrote about the misery of most citizens and the luxurious lifestyles of the ruling class that controls the poor. Outside Havana's tourist district, "the rest of the city looks as though it suffered a catastrophe on the scale of Hurricane Katrina or the Indonesian tsunami. Roofs have collapsed. Walls are splitting apart. Window glass is missing. Paint has long vanished. It's eerily dark at night, almost entirely free of automobile traffic. . . . It is filled with people struggling to eke out a life in the ruins."[12]

Free-market economies, even with their flaws, are far better than the trap of socialism.

What is "crony capitalism," and what's wrong with it?

In a free enterprise system, one of government's jobs is to make sure competing businesses all play by the same rules. Government shouldn't give some corporations special privileges and others not. Competition that's truly free and fair requires a level playing field.

Unfortunately, modern American government tends to do this

job badly. Big corporations often get too cozy with government officials. That can lead to special treatment known as "crony capitalism." Under crony capitalism, businesses (usually big corporations or groups of corporations) hire lobbyists who work to pass laws and regulations that favor those businesses. This goes on a lot in Washington, DC, in statehouses across the country, and even at the local government level.

Sometimes companies are looking for loans or grants. A corporation might go to its friends in government and say, "Look, we can create all kinds of jobs making this new product, but we'll need some help getting it off the ground. Can the government guarantee a loan for us?"

That means taxpayers are taking a risk for that company, and if it fails, taxpayers are the ones who pay. A recent well-known example is Solyndra, a solar cell manufacturing company that went bankrupt in 2011 after getting a loan guarantee from the US Department of Energy. The bankruptcy cost taxpayers hundreds of millions of dollars.

Sometimes crony capitalism involves big corporations pushing for government regulations that make it tough for new businesses to enter their line of work. In other words, they use the government to protect themselves from new competition.

Sometimes it involves corporations getting special tax breaks for themselves written into a law. There's nothing wrong with lower taxes (especially since America has one of the highest corporate tax rates in the world), but it's not fair when some businesses have to pay much more than others. And it makes people mad when they read about big corporations that manage to pay practically no taxes.

Corporations that lobby the government in their own interests aren't breaking any laws—that's part of our democratic system. And there are times when it makes sense for government to extend a helping hand, especially if it's help that can boost the economy and get people to work.

But rampant crony capitalism interferes with free enterprise, which depends on fair competition. It usually favors big corporations, which can afford to lobby government, at the expense of smaller companies. That can keep entrepreneurs from launching small businesses and creating jobs.

Crony capitalism rewards businesses based on connections and their ability to influence the government rather than the quality of their product or service. It inhibits competition, driving up the prices of goods for consumers.

Corporations shouldn't get a government-supplied edge over competitors. Government should be on the side of fair and open competition. That's the best way to foster innovation and economic growth.

EQUALITY *and* OPPORTUNITY

AN ECONOMICS PROFESSOR got tired of hearing his students say that the United States is an unfair place and that the government ought to do something to make things more equal (lessons they had apparently learned in social studies class and on TV).

"All right," the professor said. "We'll try a little experiment. From now on, all grades will be averaged. Everyone will receive the same grade, whatever that turns out to be. You can all be equal."

After the first test, he averaged all the grades, and everyone got a B. The students who had studied hard were mad, but the students who had studied only a little were happy.

As the second test approached, the students who had studied hard decided they wanted a free ride too. They didn't study as much this time. The students who had studied a little for the first test studied even less for the second. The average grade was a D. No one was happy.

When the third test rolled around, the average was an F.

As the tests proceeded, the grades never got any better. Bickering and blaming, however, were on the rise. At the end of the semester, the whole class failed.

This story, which likely falls into the category of "urban legend," appeared on the Internet several years ago.[1] Apocryphal or not, it's a great illustration for helping us think about what equality means and what conditions offer the best opportunities for true success.

What does the Declaration of Independence mean by "all men are created equal"?

Does it mean we should all get an equal start in life? No. Thomas Jefferson and the others who wrote the Declaration were realists. They knew that life isn't always fair and that people are born with different abilities. Some are born in very wealthy countries, some in impoverished countries. Even in the United States, some are born into rich families, some into poor.

"All men are created equal" means that we're all born with the same fundamental rights—the founders called them "natural rights"—such as the right to life, liberty, and the pursuit of happiness. By "all men," the founders meant all humanity, although it took many years for the country to include women and people of color in its founding vision.

The founders believed, as do most conservatives today, that these fundamental rights come from God. All people are "endowed by their Creator" with them, as the Declaration puts it.

Government is not the source of our rights, but it plays a crucial role by protecting those rights with laws. We all stand equal before the nation's laws. We expect the government to treat us all in an evenhanded manner.

"All men are created equal" carries the idea that human life is something to be cherished. Since we are created by God in his image, there is something sacred about every human being. There is a dignity built into every individual who comes into this world, and each individual life has value.

This doesn't mean everyone is worthy of equal respect. Those who regularly steal or lie or hurt others, for example, have forfeited their honor and sometimes their freedom. We certainly shouldn't esteem people like that.

It does mean, however, that each life has worth and potential. The phrase "all men are created equal" carries a moral obligation for us to treat one another with basic decency. Here in the United States we may take that idea for granted, but there are large parts of the world where it isn't in force, where life is viewed as cheap and others' rights as expendable.

Someone was once asked to summarize America in three words. "No privileged characters," he answered. That's a very American ideal. This country, at its best, is the land of equal rights and shared obligations.

Why shouldn't government close the gap between the haves and have-nots to make things equal?

Most Americans, including most conservatives, believe in policies to help narrow the gap between rich and poor in limited ways. For example, they accept the general notion of a progressive tax system in which high income earners pay a greater portion of their income to taxes than those who make less money, so long as the amount is within reason. Americans generally favor sensible programs to help raise poor people's standard of living and create opportunities for them to make more money.

The problem comes when government goes over the line and promises to make things fair by taking from some and giving to others. "Those rich people don't deserve all that money," some on the left argue. "Government should use its power to even things out."

Some nations have promised material equality, but the results have never been good. Communist governments tried it in the twentieth century and failed on a massive scale.

If you want to learn about the effects of communism, read about East Berlin and West Berlin during the Cold War. East Germany, including East Berlin, was a communist nation where everyone was supposed to share the wealth. East Berlin was a city of run-down buildings, drab stores, and crumbling roads. Families waited years for basic appliances like washing machines and refrigerators.

West Berlin was an outpost of freedom inside East Germany, protected by the United States and its allies. It was a prosperous city with busy streets, stores, and cafés. So many East Berliners wanted to go to West Berlin that the communists had to build the Berlin Wall to keep people in, and they would shoot anyone who tried to go over it.

Would you want to live in a place where the government tells you what and how much you can have? That's the only way to make things "equal" from a material standpoint. Think about what that would do to your hopes, your incentive to do your best.

Government control of wealth in the name of equality has a predictable outcome—the people running the government and their friends end up doing quite well. George Orwell painted the picture in his classic book *Animal Farm*. The animals took over the farm with the maxim "All animals are equal," but as time passed and the pigs exerted more and more control, the maxim turned into "All animals are equal, but some animals are more equal than others."

This isn't to say that government should not help people who really need it, especially those who can't care for themselves. Of course it should. Americans want to use government in smart, effective ways to help fellow Americans who are struggling. For example, government can help ensure that children from disadvantaged families have access to nutritious food and a good education. Giving people a chance to make better lives for themselves is what this country is all about.

Americans are also generous in helping without governmental involvement through churches and other charities. "Happy is he who is kind to the poor," the book of Proverbs reminds us.[2]

But leveling society in the name of equality makes the state the master and individuals its servants. As the great British prime minister Winston Churchill observed, it's a good way to bring an "equal sharing of miseries."

What does the Declaration of Independence mean by "the pursuit of happiness"?

The Declaration says we are all endowed by our Creator with the right to "life, liberty, and the pursuit of happiness." In this case, "happiness" doesn't mean being cheerful or feeling good. We have to look to other sources to help us decipher exactly what the Declaration is getting at here.

You'll often read that "the pursuit of happiness" really means "the pursuit of property." That's because the English philosopher John Locke, whose writings influenced Thomas Jefferson and other American founders, wrote of the right of man "to preserve his property, that is, his life, liberty and estate."[3]

The founders believed that property rights are crucial for human liberty. People can't be free if they don't have the right to the fruits of their own labor. The founders also believed that having a little property, such as a home and land, helps make a person independent.

By "the pursuit of happiness," Jefferson included the idea of property rights, but he meant a broader concept as well. To understand it, we need to turn to the ancient Greeks, whom Jefferson had studied.

The Greek word for happiness was *eudaimonia*, which includes the idea of personal well-being or flourishing. To the Greeks, being happy meant living a good life, not just in the sense of being comfortable and safe but also in living a virtuous life. A person can't be truly happy without virtues such as self-control, honesty, and courage.

The ancient Greeks also connected happiness with fulfilling one's potential. A good lyre player, for example, is happy when playing the lyre well. A computer scientist is happy working with computers, and a businessperson is happy making business deals. In other words, one's chosen work can bring happiness—whether it's paying work, volunteer work, or work at being a father or mother.

The idea of the American Dream is connected to the idea of the pursuit of happiness. The American Dream means much more than owning a house, a car, and a big flat-screen TV. It means the chance to follow a dream, to work hard at turning a vision into something real.

If Jefferson were alive today, he might say that "the pursuit of happiness" is something like the opportunity to reach one's fullest potential. The Declaration says we all have the God-given right to use our abilities to go as far as we can. There is no guarantee of a good life, but in America there is the opportunity to strive for one morally, intellectually, and economically.

What makes America the "land of opportunity"?

There is no single ingredient to the formula. It's a mixture of several things.

The first is liberty, including economic freedom. That freedom allows people to choose their own careers and put their talents to work. It allows them to profit from their own ideas and labor, to work for themselves if they want.

Abraham Lincoln said, "This progress by which the poor, honest, industrious, and resolute man raises himself, that he may work on his own account, and hire somebody else . . . is the great principle for which this government was really formed."[4]

Limited government that protects rights and freedoms is another important ingredient. For example, it is government's job to protect property rights, keep markets as free and fair as possible, and oppose discrimination in the workplace. Too much government, on the other hand, weighs down the economy with high taxes and costly regulations. That kills opportunity for individuals and businesses.

National character is a third ingredient. The American spirit values business. It prizes inventiveness, entrepreneurship, and hard work. It also values education—Americans have always believed that education and opportunity go together.

The moral character of the American people is crucial—virtues like dealing honestly with others, wanting to do good work, and taking personal responsibility. Where those virtues don't exist, opportunity doesn't last.

Families make a big difference. Family is the first and most important teacher of the character needed for success. It's where we first learn the virtues that go into making a healthy work ethic, virtues such as integrity, dedication, and perseverance. Talk to people who have had success, and they often say things like "My dad taught me to never quit" or "My mom made me believe I could do it."

Finally, strong communities are essential. Vibrant neighborhoods, churches, and civic groups like the local chamber of commerce or Lions Club are places where opportunity thrives. They form networks where you can look for jobs, build a reputation, and develop business relationships. These institutions, plus families, are the backbone of American opportunity.

How do we increase opportunity in America?

A lot of people worry that opportunity in America is on the decline. They worry that many of us don't have a good chance to climb the ladder of success and that it will be even tougher for coming generations.

Those on the left often say, "Let's fix things by taking money from the rich and redistributing it through government programs." But taking more money from wealthy people has a poor record in terms of increasing opportunity. It may satisfy envy or some people's sense of fairness, but income redistribution has done little to give people tools for long-term success.[5]

One good way to increase opportunity is to strengthen the foundations of the economy. The better the economy, the better your chances of getting a good job. That does more for upward mobility than any big government program.

Government can help fuel economic growth with policies that support free enterprise and don't slow businesses down with too much regulation. Improving education and combating the breakdown of the American family are crucial long-term strategies as well.

The best way to improve opportunity in America may be something that doesn't involve government at all. It's a formula for getting ahead called the "success sequence." Social scientists, economists, and people with common sense have known about it for a long time. Follow these steps in the right order, and your chances of getting ahead are good.

Here's the sequence: 1) Finish high school. A college degree is even better, but at least finish high school. 2) Get a job. It doesn't have to be a dream job you'll have forever—simply a full-time job, one you're qualified for. 3) Get married. Yes, marriage is good for financial success. 4) Have babies and start to raise them *after* you get married.

That's it. Get an education, get a job, get married, and start a family, in that order. If everybody in America followed this path, studies show that the poverty rate would plummet.[6] Stick to that sequence, and you vastly increase your access to the American Dream.

This solution calls for personal responsibility. Following the "success sequence" is easier said than done—steps like finishing a degree and getting a job are big ones. They take perseverance. Keeping a marriage healthy and raising children are even bigger challenges. But if more Americans get back to following that route, this country will still be the land of opportunity.

ENERGY *and the*
ENVIRONMENT

THE FIRST EARTH DAY was observed in 1970. It was, in the words of famed CBS anchorman Walter Cronkite, "a day set aside for a nationwide outpouring of mankind seeking its own survival." Its message about saving the earth was simple: "Act or die."[1]

Around that time, news reports were full of catastrophic warnings:

"Colder Winters Herald Dawn of New Ice Age—Scientists See Ice Age in the Future"
—HEADLINE FROM THE *Washington Post*, JANUARY 11, 1970[2]

"Dr. S. Dillon Ripley, secretary of the Smithsonian Institute, believes that in 25 years, somewhere between 75 and 80 percent of all the species of living animals will be extinct."
—SENATOR GAYLORD NELSON, *Look* MAGAZINE, APRIL 1970

"By 1985 air pollution will have reduced the amount of sunlight reaching earth by one half."
—*Life* MAGAZINE, JANUARY 1970

"By the year 2000, if present trends continue, we will be using up crude oil at such a rate . . . that there won't be any more crude oil. You'll drive up to the pump and say, 'Fill 'er up, buddy,' and he'll say, 'I am very sorry, there isn't any.'"
—ECOLOGIST KENNETH WATT, *Time* MAGAZINE, FEBRUARY 2, 1970[3]

None of those predictions came true, but the alarmists' warnings have continued for decades now. A 2014 Earth Day Network website told us,

> The fight against climate change is at an impasse and life on Earth hangs in the balance. Help us save polar bears and other wildlife as their habitats disappear and their food sources become scarce. Like the polar bear, human life is under threat, too. Storms are becoming stronger, droughts are becoming more severe, and rising sea levels encroach on our cities.[4]

Protecting the environment is serious business, but dire statements like these aren't. This is an area where you have to be skeptical of radical claims, examine the evidence, and use common sense.

Energy, environmental, and free enterprise issues are tightly intertwined. Free enterprise, after all, requires building, trading, and moving things. That consumes energy and affects the environment. It takes some thoughtful balancing to encourage economic growth, look after the earth, and use energy wisely. It also makes for lively political debate.

Why don't conservatives care about the environment?

A listener to Bill Bennett's *Morning in America* recently called from Tampa Bay, Florida, to describe an environmental studies lesson in his son's high school. The teacher treated the students to a PowerPoint presentation on "Environmental History" showing a picture of President Ronald Reagan with a speech bubble containing the words "I hate Earth!" coming out of his mouth. That's a message some liberals want people to believe: conservatives don't care about the environment.

It's an absurd claim. Nobody wants to breathe dirty air or drink foul water. Conservatives want to preserve the environment for future generations as much as anyone else. *Conservation* and *conservatism* share the same Latin root *conservare*, meaning to preserve and keep safe.

Unlike radical environmentalists, conservatives don't believe that human activity is essentially bad for the planet. They support good stewardship of the earth while putting its resources to work in smart, efficient ways that benefit people.

Environmentalism has done much good for the world, and sensible laws are certainly necessary to help protect the earth. But some environmentalists are so zealous, they forget to take people's well-being into account.

Their views about energy are a good example. Radical environmentalists are up in arms about oil wells and oil pipelines. They condemn drilling for natural gas, especially hydraulic fracking. They don't like coal-burning plants, even ones that use clean coal technology. They oppose construction of nuclear plants. But people need energy, and without any of those options we'd all be in very bad shape.

People in poor, developing countries especially need such energy. More than 1.2 billion people around the world lack access to electricity. Another 2.8 billion use fuels like wood, charcoal, and animal dung to cook—fuels that have negative health and environmental consequences.[5] Ironic as it may seem, the modern hydrocarbon energy that environmentalists so dislike is the path to cleaner, healthier conditions in the developing world.

The most extreme environmentalists are anti-business and anti-economic development. They believe that free enterprise and industrialism are natural enemies of the environment. Many are socialists at heart; they think that free enterprise is inherently unfair because it leaves some people with more than others. They use environmental regulations to limit commerce and grow centralized government.

Conservatives believe that free enterprise, used wisely, can go hand in hand with preserving the environment. New technologies made possible by free enterprise can be used to solve environmental problems. For example, improved automobile technology has reduced tailpipe emissions by 95 percent since 1970.[6] Good stewardship of the earth and its resources, not an anti-people, anti-business attitude, is the sensible approach to take.

Is oil evil?

No. On balance, oil and other fossil fuels have brought tremendous improvements to people's lives. They've made it possible to feed, clothe, house, and transport billions. Search online for "list of petroleum-based products" and take a look. It's virtually everything we use around our homes, offices, and schools, from deodorant to computer parts to medicines.

Some on the left have turned oil into a symbol of everything they don't like about Western culture and capitalism in particular. To them, oil, natural gas, and coal stand for pollution and global warming (or "climate change," as it's often called). Oil equals capitalism and industrialization, which equal inequality and environmental wreckage. The left often paints "big oil" as a bunch of greedy, callous corporations out to wreck the planet for profit.

It's not an accurate or fair portrayal. Oil companies aren't perfect—no corporations are—and there was a time when they were bad about taking care of the environment. But times have changed, and people in the industry generally do a good job of using new technologies to minimize the impact on the earth while providing a valuable service. For example, oil and gas companies can now drill sideways, which allows them to drill several wells in different directions from one spot, leaving a smaller "footprint" on the surface.

The bottom line is this: at present there is no workable replacement for fossil fuels. The world needs them to keep economies going. "Green" alternatives like solar and wind power are too inefficient, unreliable, and costly to take their place anytime soon.

Someday technology advances will surely make fossil fuels unnecessary, but for the foreseeable future, we need them. Without fossil fuels, the world would face economic depression and mass starvation.

Not long ago, "experts" were predicting that the world would soon run out of fossil fuels. What they didn't foresee was that new technologies would make vast oil and natural gas fields accessible. Thanks to that technology, the United States became the world's leading natural gas producer in 2010 and leading oil producer in 2014.[7]

America needs to develop all its available energy sources, including its oil and gas fields, and to do it in a responsible way. Those resources create jobs and play a big role in keeping the economy healthy. They help keep transportation costs down and reduce dependence on foreign oil. Using resources wisely, always considering the environment, makes more sense than demonizing them.

Isn't it nuts to be skeptical about global warming?

When it comes to new scientific ideas, skepticism is a healthy attitude to take. In fact, good science demands the kind of skepticism that says, "Show me some proof." As the late astronomer Carl Sagan used to say, extraordinary claims require extraordinary evidence.

We shouldn't simply reject out of hand the idea that human activity is causing dangerous global warming—the implications are too serious. By the same token, we shouldn't accept the idea of global warming just because others say so.

The left has gone to great lengths to persuade people *not* to question the idea. We're told that the debate is over, that man-caused global warming is a fact, that the results will definitely be catastrophic unless we do something about it. Skeptics are called "deniers" (an epithet similar to "Holocaust deniers," people who deny that genocide against Jews took place during World War II).

For example, former vice president Al Gore has likened "raging deniers" to racists, supporters of apartheid, slaveholders, homophobes, and alcoholics.[8] Environmental activist Robert F. Kennedy Jr. has said that politicians who say that global warming doesn't exist are "contemptible human beings" and that "I wish there were a law you could punish them under."[9]

It's worth remembering that when people try to shut down debate, it's often a sign they don't think they can win that debate.

Here are some questions worth investigating before making up your mind on this issue. Is the earth in fact warming? If so, by how much? Has it warmed and cooled in times past? Do we really know what causes warming? Is it definitely attributable to man? Have past predictions about climate changes been accurate?

Lots of money and politics are mixed into this issue—people saying, "We need to spend billions on this" and "We need to pass laws about that." Any time money and politics are involved, it's definitely smart to ask questions.

Is the science on global warming really settled?

It's by no means settled, despite what climate change activists and liberal politicians would have you believe. They often say things like "97 percent of the world's scientists agree that climate change is real, man-made, and dangerous." In fact, there is no reliable survey of scientists showing that 97 percent believe that.[10]

For every claim that scientists agree about the causes and dangers of global warming, you can find a claim that they don't agree. For example, one study found that only 36 percent of professional geo-scientists and engineers believe that global warming is mainly caused by humans and is dangerous.[11]

Here's what scientists do seem to agree about. There is complete agreement that "climate change" is happening. That's simply because the earth's climate is always changing—throughout history, it has always been warming or cooling. There is broad agreement that the world's climate warmed during the twentieth century. There is also broad agreement that humans affect the climate. With so many people, cars, factories, engines, and other machines on earth, it's difficult to see how we could not affect it in some way.

Beyond that, the consensus breaks down. There is no widespread agreement on crucial points like how much the earth may continue to warm, what causes warming, how much of a role human activity plays, and what sort of threat warming might pose.

Dr. Steven E. Koonin is a distinguished theoretical physicist who served as undersecretary for science at the US Department of Energy during the Obama administration. He takes the issue of climate change seriously. Like many scientists, he regards claims of climate science being settled as, to use his word, "misguided." As he points out, the earth's climate is incredibly complex, and scientists don't fully understand it. That makes it very hard to predict what it will be like in coming decades and how much human activity will affect it. Dr. Koonin writes,

While the past two decades have seen progress in climate science, the field is not yet mature enough to usefully answer the difficult and important questions being asked of it. This decidedly unsettled state highlights what should be obvious: Understanding climate, at the level of detail relevant to human influences, is a very, very difficult problem.[12]

Those who claim that the "science is settled" on this issue are making a political statement to suit their agenda. They are being anything but scientific.

What are some problems with global warming theories?

The main problem with the theory that humans are causing dangerous global warming is that scientists don't understand enough about the complexities of the earth's climate to draw firm conclusions or make predictions with anything near certainty. There are several specific problems as well. Here are four:

- **The climate has been warming and cooling for ages.** There is no doubt about that. The earth's climate has gone through cycles of warming and cooling since long before the factories and cars of the industrial age came along. This raises an obvious and common-sense question: Are the climate changes we see today simply part of a natural process that has been going on for a very long time?
- **We don't really know how humans influence the climate.** Projections are that human activity will add enough carbon dioxide to the atmosphere by the middle of the twenty-first century to directly shift its natural greenhouse effect by only 1 to 2 percent.[13] It's extremely difficult for anyone to say what such a small change means for the climate. Since we don't

fully understand the natural causes of climate change, it's virtually impossible for scientists to know how much human activity really affects it.

- **Global warming computer models don't match a lot of what's going on in the world around us.** For example, global warming has basically come to a halt for the better part of two decades, despite computer models' predictions. The models also failed to predict record-high growth of Antarctic sea ice. They fail to explain why seventy years ago seas were rising at the same rate they are today, even though human influence on the climate was smaller then.[14]

- **Global warming has become a non-falsifiable theory.** People who insist that it's a human-caused threat tend to point to just about everything as evidence. When the climate warms, it's because of global warming. When the climate doesn't warm, it's merely a "pause." Warm winters, cold winters, floods, droughts, lots of snow, little snow, severe storms—they're all said to be results of global warming. Everything proves it; nothing disproves it. That's called a non-falsifiable theory. At that point global warming is an ideology, not science.

News reports about global warming rarely mention these problems with the theory. In fact, they tend to ignore them.[15]

For example, journalists regularly write stories announcing that the previous year was "the hottest year ever" or "one of the warmest ever recorded." What most of those stories don't tell you is that such claims are based on temperature readings taken at the earth's surface, which are not always reliable, and that the recorded temperature increases are so small, it's hard to tell if they mean anything at all. The stories also don't tell you that atmospheric temperatures measured by satellites—which offer a more reliable measurement—show no evidence of significant warming in recent years.[16]

Global warming activists haven't helped their cause with shrill predictions over the years. For example, in 1989 a senior official at the United Nations predicted that "entire nations could be wiped off the face of Earth by rising sea levels if the global-warming trend is not reversed by the year 2000." He also predicted that "coastal flooding and crop failures would create an exodus of 'eco-refugees,' threatening political chaos."[17] Prophecies like that have turned out to be nothing more than hot greenhouse gas.

Even if we're not sure about global warming, doesn't it make sense to play it safe and cut back on greenhouse gas emissions?

If "playing it safe" means enacting sensible policies about using energy cleanly and efficiently and developing new energy sources, the answer is yes. But if "playing it safe" means the United States should slow industrialization, impose carbon taxes on people and businesses, spend lots of government money on inefficient "green energies," and slash the use of oil and other fossil fuels with no viable alternatives in sight, most conservatives say no. Here's why.

Government policies that say, "We're going to use taxes and regulations to force everyone to cut back on fossil fuel use" hurt the US economy. Those policies result in more expensive energy, which costs jobs and drives up the cost of goods. That makes life harder for people.

Even if the United States took on the tremendous expense of significantly cutting back greenhouse gas emissions, it would have no effect on climate change. That's because developing countries like China and India produce large amounts of greenhouse gas. They depend largely on coal and other fossil fuels to grow their economies. No matter what the United States does, developing countries have little interest in slowing down their energy use, for understandable reasons.

Cutting greenhouse emissions in developing countries would hurt people there. Many of those countries are focused on lifting people out of poverty—supplying them with basics like electricity and drinkable water. Pushing them off fossil fuels makes their energy more expensive, and that means less food, less electricity, more disease, shorter lives, and prolonged poverty.

You should understand that for many liberals, the issue of climate change is a way to expand the power of government in order to reshape the world to fit their vision. As one global warming activist has written, "The climate crisis is precisely the giant lever with which we can, following Archimedes, move the world in a greener, more equitable direction."[18]

Liberals are saying, in effect, "Trust us: government needs to tax your energy use more. Government needs to regulate the kind and amount of energy you use to save the world from disaster." That gives government an astounding amount of control over economies and people's lives.

Being attentive to the health of the environment is one thing. Using predictions of climate catastrophe to drive a left-wing political agenda is another.

Part 2

LIMITED
GOVERNMENT

LIMITED GOVERNMENT

CONGRESSMAN PAUL RYAN OF Wisconsin tells the story of Chrissy, a constituent who was seventeen years old and very sick when he first met her. She had a life-threatening heart condition and needed a special pacemaker.

The device was available in Europe, and a company was willing to send it from France. But there was a big catch. The US government had not approved the device for use here.

Chrissy's mom did everything she could to get a waiver from the Food and Drug Administration so she could get the pacemaker into the country, with no success. Her request was trapped somewhere in the bureaucracy. Meanwhile, Chrissy's life was ebbing away.

With nowhere else to turn, Chrissy's mom walked into Congressman Ryan's district office in Wisconsin crying. Ryan managed to get the head of the FDA on the phone and told him he would not take no for an answer. Fifteen minutes later, the FDA called back. The waiver would be approved.

"Today, Chrissy is a nurse and living a full life, but what about all of the other people trapped in—or turned away by—our growing federal bureaucracy?" Ryan asks.[1]

This is the heart of the question. Is a huge, bloated government that holds so much power over our lives really one that helps people the most? Or is it slowly draining away the strengths and ideals that have made this country great?

One thing is for certain: it is not the kind of government this nation's founders had in mind.

Do conservatives hate government?

No, conservatives don't hate government, despite what the media and liberals sometimes imply. People who don't want government are anarchists, not conservatives.

Conservatives are opposed to *big* government that overtaxes and overregulates—the kind of government that, as the late British prime minister Margaret Thatcher used to say, takes too much from you in order to do too much for you. They're opposed to bad government that wastes money and runs poorly.

But conservatives are certainly not opposed to government in general. Government "of the people, by the people, for the people," as Abraham Lincoln put it in the Gettysburg Address, is a good thing. We all need government to carry out responsibilities such as making and enforcing laws, protecting people's rights, and defending us from foreign enemies. We need it to do things like protect the environment and make sure the food we buy is safe to eat.

Conservatives are proud of the system of *limited government* that America gave the world with the United States Constitution in 1787. Our Constitution is still a miracle of sorts. It is arguably the greatest political document in history. It created a new kind of government, one that did away with the tyranny of kings. President Ronald Reagan put it this way in his farewell address to the nation in 1989:

> Ours was the first revolution in the history of mankind
> that truly reversed the course of government, and with
> three little words: "We the People." "We the People" tell
> the government what to do; it doesn't tell us. "We the
> People" are the driver; the government is the car. And we
> decide where it should go, and by what route, and how
> fast. Almost all the world's constitutions are documents
> in which governments tell the people what their privileges
> are. Our Constitution is a document in which "We the
> People" tell the government what it is allowed to do.[2]

Conservatives want a federal government that actually listens to "We the People." They want government that is vigorous about helping people solve problems instead of burdening them with more regulations and bureaucracy. They want a strong government but a limited one; they want a limited government but strong.

Conservatives want the federal government to be especially strong in jobs that only it can do, like providing for the country's defense. As Alexander Hamilton put it, "Whenever the government appears in arms, it ought to appear like a *Hercules* and inspire respect by the display of strength."[3]

There are many jobs it makes sense for the federal government to take part in, like providing a "safety net" for the poor and help for elderly Americans who need it. For those important tasks, conservatives want smart, energetic government that gets the job right. What they *don't* want is government that spends a lot, wastes a lot, and in the end gets poor results for rich and poor alike.

What does "limited government" mean?

Limited government is government restricted in power. It's powerful enough to protect people's God-given liberty and other inalienable rights. It's energetic enough to help make the country a better place and ensure that we all have opportunities to thrive. But it's not so powerful that it threatens our rights and squelches opportunity.

The country's founders tried hard to restrict the government's power with the checks and balances they built into the system, like giving the president power to veto bills passed by Congress. They also tried to make sure that power would be divided between the federal and state governments.

Why did the founders want to limit government? They were students of human nature and history. They knew that there are people who love to wield power over others. As Samuel Adams put it, "Ambition and lust of power above the law are . . . predominant passions in the breasts of most men."[4]

The founders also knew that over time, governments have a tendency to amass power. For most of the world's history, after all, people had lived under rulers who grabbed all the power they could get.

If government's power is unrestricted, it will naturally grow and control more of people's lives. According to Thomas Jefferson, "The natural progress of things is for liberty to yield, and government to gain ground."[5]

Abraham Lincoln left us with a good description of limited government. He wrote, "The legitimate object of government is to do for a community of people whatever they need to have done but cannot do at all, or cannot so well do for themselves in their separate and individual capacities. In all that the people can individually do as well for themselves, government ought not to interfere."[6]

Do we have limited government in the United States today?

No. It keeps growing like a snowball rolling down a hill toward Hades, to paraphrase a country song.

It started out small. When Thomas Jefferson was the secretary of state, for example, he had seven employees working at the State Department. Today the federal government employs around 2.7 million civil servants.[7] That number doesn't count uniformed members of the armed forces or legions of private contract workers the government hires. Altogether federal, state, and local governments in the United States employ about twenty-two million people.[8]

Federal bureaucracies issue more than 3,500 new regulations every year, affecting everything from the clothes we wear to the schools we attend to the television shows we watch.[9] The *Federal Register*, the official journal containing US government rules, is about eighty thousand pages long.[10] As the chart below shows, the government keeps piling regulations onto the American people.

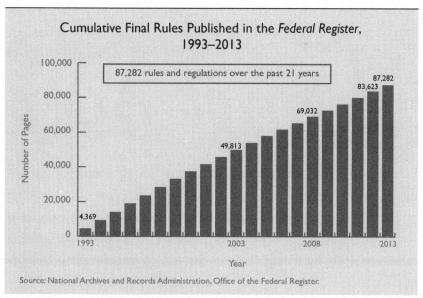

Graph courtesy of the Competitive Enterprise Institute

To be fair, much of government's expansion is due to the growth of the country's population and changes in the world. In George Washington's day, we didn't face issues like dealing with Islamic terrorism or the disposal of nuclear waste materials.

But much growth has come from the government taking more and more power for itself, just as the founders feared. Many officials in Washington, DC, think they know better than people living in places like Iowa and Alabama. They believe they should wield power because they have superior wisdom and expertise.

In truth, there is no special wisdom that comes from being in Washington, DC. Working in the nation's capital doesn't make you smarter or more knowledgeable than Americans elsewhere. Yet a "we know what's best for you" mind-set is often the way the federal government acts.

Many politicians go to Washington pledging to cut the size of government programs, but that almost never happens. Washington is full of lobbyists representing groups that want money, services, or regulations from the government, and they often get what they want. Laws get stuffed with so many goodies for different groups that lawmakers often aren't sure what's in the legislation they pass. Once a government program is born, it's almost impossible to get rid of—it just keeps growing and growing.

Who made government so big and powerful?

Ultimately, the American people themselves are responsible for government growing so much. In election after election, they have voted for politicians who supported expanding government. Many people, it seems, are for smaller government in theory but accept larger government in reality. They're in favor of cutting government programs but not if it means cutting any programs that benefit them personally. Both political parties, Democrat and Republican, have had a hand in growing government. Liberals (whether Democrats or Republicans) are the main supporters of big government. Liberals' solutions to problems almost always mean more government programs and more government spending.

To understand how government got so big, it helps to know a little history.

Government expansion began in earnest with the Progressive movement in the late nineteenth and early twentieth centuries. Progressive reformers like Theodore Roosevelt and Woodrow Wilson believed that the founders' vision of limited government was outdated. They argued that in an age of industrialization and giant corporations that could take advantage of people, government needed to fashion a more just society. As Woodrow Wilson wrote, "Government does now whatever experience permits or the times demand."[11]

Government grew even larger in the 1930s under President Franklin D. Roosevelt's New Deal. Roosevelt believed that because of the Great Depression, the federal government needed to do much more to regulate the economy and improve people's living conditions. He set up a raft of agencies like the Securities and Exchange Commission and the Works Progress Administration. Under the New Deal, power shifted from state and local governments to Washington, DC.

In the 1960s, President Lyndon B. Johnson's Great Society agenda expanded government even more. The Great Society's aim was to bring an "end to poverty and racial injustice" as well as "enrich and elevate our national life."[12] Johnson launched programs that included funding for schools, job training for the unemployed, housing projects to replace slums, food stamps for the needy, money to encourage the arts, and Medicare and Medicaid, which provide health care for the elderly and the poor.

More recently, President Barack Obama's Affordable Care Act (often called "Obamacare") pushed government even deeper into daily life. It gives government much more control over America's health care system.

Today the federal government runs more programs, spends more money, and wields more power than ever. Its influence over Americans' lives would stun men like James Madison and Thomas Jefferson.

What's so bad about big government?

The federal government is so huge and bloated, it creates all sorts of problems:

- **Big government is wildly expensive.** Washington spends a massive amount of money. In 2014, it spent about $3.5 trillion. It borrowed about fourteen cents out of every dollar spent.[13] It has racked up $18 trillion in debt, a number that keeps rising. That comes to nearly $60,000 of debt for every American.[14] No one knows how that money will be repaid.

  Federal regulations are also extremely expensive. Businesses must build the cost of complying with regulations into the price of goods and services they sell. When you buy something, whether it be a loaf of bread or a cell phone, you help pay for those regulations. According to one estimate, regulations cost each American household, on average, about $15,000 per year.[15] Some people believe we are getting to the point where we will not be able to curb big government's spending habits. If that happens, the country may well go broke.

- **Bureaucracy is inefficient and wasteful.** Stories of government waste are so common, people barely notice them anymore. In 2014, for example, the Social Security Administration revealed that it had spent six years and nearly $300 million on a computer system that didn't work.[16] In 2013, the Interior Department spent nearly $100,000 to install an outhouse with one toilet and no plumbing on an Alaskan trail. The National Institutes of Health spent over $335,000 on a study to find out if married couples are happier if wives calm down quickly after an argument. (They are.)[17]

- **Fraud and abuse can be a big problem.** For example, Medicare and Medicaid—huge programs that pay for health care for the elderly and poor—have rampant problems with health care providers overbilling the government. No one even knows how much abuse is involved. It may be as high as $100 billion a year or more.

  With so many programs paying out so much money, people are bound to take advantage. The government reports billions of dollars in "improper" unemployment payments every year. Investigations by the Social Security Administration have turned up massive fraud by people faking or exaggerating disabilities to get money.[18]

- **Many programs don't work well or at all.** They keep going anyway and even get bigger. Head Start is a good example. Launched in 1965, Head Start is a preschool program for children from low-income families. Its goal is to help those children get ready for elementary school. Around one million children are enrolled in the program each year.

  Despite its intentions, Head Start does little if any good when it comes to education. According to a study released by the US Department of Health and Human Services, the program has no lasting effects on children's achievement in school.[19] Yet Head Start costs around $8 billion per year. Ironically, it is a very popular program.

- **Big government can stifle the economy.** Dealing with excessive regulation costs time and money. It slows businesses and chokes opportunities.

  The late George McGovern, a well-known liberal senator

from South Dakota, learned that lesson the hard way. After retiring from the US Senate, he followed a dream of operating a hotel. McGovern quickly learned how much time and money it takes to deal with government regulations. "It is a simple concern that is nonetheless often ignored by legislators," he wrote.[20] He realized that if he had known what it was like to be a businessman before he was a senator, he would not have supported so many regulations.

- **Big government poses risks to freedom.** This may be the most damaging effect of all. More than half of Americans surveyed say that the federal government threatens their personal rights and freedoms.[21] That view would surely discourage the founders, who set out to design a government to *protect* people's rights.

  Government is so big that it has something to say about virtually every aspect of our lives. Federal rules determine how much water our toilets use and what kind of light-bulbs we screw into our lamps. They dictate what kind of ingredients go into our food and what kind of mileage our cars get.

Laws are necessary, of course. They help make sure the meat we buy is safe and our rivers are clean. But the larger and more powerful government becomes, the more control it has over our lives. The question is, where do we cross the line from being the land of the free to becoming a land of government decree?

Is it possible to check government's growth?

Yes, if enough people understand and respect the principle of limited government. Here are a few questions to ask when someone starts talking about government doing more:

- **Is a proposed law or program truly needed?** Many laws get passed not because of real need but because of something someone wants, like money for a pet project. If a bill or expenditure is not related to a basic function of government, it deserves extra scrutiny.
- **How much is a proposed law or regulation going to cost?** How is it going to be paid for? Government officials are notorious for underestimating how much programs will cost. If you hear them throw out a number, you can often double or even triple it to get an idea of the true cost.
- **Could a proposed law be handled better at the local or state level than at the federal level?** As a general rule, the closer a government is to the people, the better it knows what kind of laws people want and what sort of laws will work in that place.
- **Can the private sector handle this better than the public sector?** Businesses are usually more efficient, quicker, and more innovative at solving problems than government is. Likewise, nonprofit organizations and volunteer agencies are often better at helping people than government.
- **Is a proposed law too vague?** The US Congress has gotten into the habit of passing vague laws that leave the details up to government agencies to decide. This opens the door for unelected officials in the bureaucracy to issue more and more regulations. Vague laws also lead to lawsuits and judges having to decide what the laws really mean.
- **Does a proposed law respect the idea of personal responsibility?** Is it setting government up to take over an obligation that people really should be taking care of themselves? If so, then red flags should be flying.

At the end of the day, the American people have to avoid the mistake of thinking that government has a solution for every problem.

Yes, government has important jobs to do. But a free republic needs citizens who take responsibility for themselves and their families and who help their neighbors and communities instead of always looking to big government for answers.

What's the alternative to big government?

The alternative is smarter, better government.

Yes, conservatives want to limit government's growth and cut it back where possible. They want to stop out-of-control spending and borrowing in Washington, DC. They're in favor of taking a close look at government operations and asking questions like "Is this program really working?" and "Do we really need it?"

But conservatives also recognize that modern government has much important work to do, from providing a safety net for the poor to keeping air travel safe. Conservatives want to improve government while limiting it. They want to streamline it and make it more responsive to people's needs.

Conservatives don't want to eliminate government. They want to reform it. Instead of government that says, "Here is a pile of regulations to tell you how you have to do things," they want government that asks, "What can we do to help people and businesses thrive?"

For example, over the last several decades the federal government has taken more and more control of America's health care system. The more control it has taken, the higher health care costs have shot. Conservatives want government to protect Americans with laws that ensure they have access to good health care, but they also want less government control of health care markets. They want to use the power of free markets to make health care more affordable.

Tax reform is another example. The US tax code contains nearly four million words. It's a tangled net of rules, rates, deductions, and exemptions. Altogether Americans spend billions of hours and dollars every year to prepare their returns.[22] Conservatives want a simplified, straightforward tax system that people can actually understand, one that adequately funds the government, aids the poor, and helps the middle class thrive.

The federal government is like a big, clunky machine with thousands of parts. Some of the parts don't work very well, but we keep adding more pieces to keep the machine rumbling along. We add more and more government, thinking that will make things better.

There's a smarter way. Think of a cell phone or tablet. Over the years, those devices haven't grown bigger and more clunky. They've gotten sleeker, nimbler, and more user friendly. They put users in control with different apps and options to choose from. They're designed to help people create things, meet challenges, and solve problems. Each new version gives more bang for the buck.

That's the direction the world of technology keeps moving. Government should do the same.

Where should we look for solutions, if not to big government?

Government can and should help solve problems, but Washington, DC, or the state capital shouldn't be the first place we automatically turn. If we do, we're likely to be disappointed.

The conservative vision is one of Americans helping each other. It's a vision of energetic communities of people working together to solve problems and build better lives—not waiting a long time, often in vain, for big government to fix things.

Imagine for a minute that you're in trouble or have a problem you need help solving. Are you going to pull out your phone and call an agency in Washington, DC, to come solve it for you? No, you're probably going to turn to people close to you—perhaps family, or members of your church, or neighbors, or maybe local government. People in your community.

That's how we live, grow, and thrive best—not as isolated individuals but as members of a community of some kind. That's how America has prospered over the years: people using their freedom to band together, get things done, and help others.

Alexis de Tocqueville, a French political philosopher who visited the young United States in 1831 and published his impressions in the classic *Democracy in America*, wrote that Americans were "forever forming associations" to get things done. "Americans combine to give fetes, found seminaries, build churches, distribute books and send missionaries to the antipodes," he wrote. "Hospitals, prisons and schools take shape in that way."[23]

That spirit of pitching in, cooperating, and helping each other has always been a great strength of our country. Go to any thriving community in the United States, and you'll find groups of people working together to improve society—families, churches, synagogues, charities, neighborhood associations, businesses, chambers of commerce, civic clubs, and so on.

The eighteenth-century British statesman Edmund Burke called such groups "little platoons." Modern academics call them "mediating institutions." They mean the same thing—groups of people working together of their own free will to help each other and strengthen community.

Conservatives believe in a strong role for the "little platoons" of society. They exist in the space between the individual and the government where we live our lives. They are the groups on whose back society moves.[24]

In the last few decades, big government has tried to take over and crowd out some of the work of the "little platoons." It hasn't worked well. Big government agencies don't do a good job of filling in for families and communities.

The conservative vision is one of people coming together to help each other without government running the show. The more that happens, the stronger and more vibrant our democracy becomes.

That's not an unrealistic vision. It's something Americans know how to do well. What's unrealistic is a mind-set that assumes the federal government can take the lead in making our lives better for us.

Where does government come in?

Government plays an important role in this mix. It does necessary things like providing defense at the national level and maintaining roads at the state and local levels. It also helps people, but not by producing mounds of regulations and trying to manage people's lives.

Government can help make sure everyone gets a fair chance and plays by the same rules. It can help communities work on projects and ideas that improve lives. It can lend a hand to help people up and provide aid to those who need it most. Government should do all these things in a supporting role, not a controlling one.

Conservatives believe in what's called the principle of subsidiarity. It holds that a problem is usually best solved by local institutions closest to the problem. They know the conditions best and have the most interest in fixing things. The principle of subsidiarity recognizes that the knowledge and skill to address problems is spread out all over the country, not held by just a few all-knowing experts in Washington, DC.

Solving a problem is usually a face-to-face effort; it takes people working directly with each other. Distant, faceless bureaucracies in Washington usually aren't the best solution. Their intentions may be good, but to big government agencies, problems in far-off parts of the country are about as personal as numbers on a page. It's almost impossible for the federal government to come up with policies that fit the lives of more than 300 million people.

The bottom-up process of solving problems and improving lives works best. Responsibility for action should lie with the group closest to the problem—families, community groups, local governments, and state governments. If the closest group can't get it done, then help can come from the next level up. Federal government should be the last resort, not the first.

In fact, when big government tries to do too much, it makes people less energetic about improving their communities. It leads them into a habit of thinking that somebody else will eventually come along to fix things. As de Tocqueville wrote, "The more government takes the place of associations, the more will individuals lose the idea of forming associations and need the government to come to their help."[25]

The bottom-up approach requires a lot of responsibility—individuals taking responsibility for their own actions and families taking responsibility for raising their children. It requires people fulfilling their duties to neighbors, community, and country. The performance of those duties makes society work and, ultimately, makes the United States a great nation.

THE WELFARE STATE

Welcome to "The Life of Julia." At age three, Julia enters the federal Head Start preschool program to get ready for school. By age seventeen, she's the product of a high school that's in a federal education improvement program. At age eighteen, she qualifies for federal student aid so her family can afford college.

At age twenty-two, while in college, Julia undergoes surgery covered by her parents' insurance, thanks to federal health care reform. At twenty-five, after college, she makes monthly payments on her federal student loans. At twenty-seven, she can focus on her work as a web designer rather than worry about her health because the federal government requires her insurance to cover "birth control and preventive care."

At age thirty-one, Julia decides to have a child. (We don't know who the father is, because no men appear in "The Life of Julia.") While pregnant, she gets checkups and free screenings under federal health care laws. At thirty-seven, she sends her son to a kindergarten that has "better facilities and great teachers" because of federal programs.

At forty-two, Julia starts her own web business, thanks to a federal loan program. At sixty-five, she enrolls in Medicare, the federal health insurance program for older Americans. At sixty-seven, she retires and the federal government begins sending Social Security checks, which allow her to volunteer in a community garden.

"The Life of Julia" was a fictional cartoon slide-show commercial shown on the Internet by President Barack Obama's campaign when he ran for reelection in 2012. The aim was to illustrate how the modern welfare state, as envisioned by liberals such as President Obama, can provide a secure, comfortable life.

The commercial backfired with many Americans who saw it, especially conservatives. It left them asking, "Do we want government that is *everywhere*? Do we really want each stage of our lives tied to a big government program?"

Yet many others seemed to accept this liberal vision of a welfare state that takes care of people from cradle to grave. They helped reelect President Obama to a second term.

Are Americans now comfortable living in a modern welfare state that supplies so many government benefits? Or have government programs become so bloated, expensive, and intrusive that it's time to say, "Enough"?

What is the "welfare state"?

In a welfare state, government assumes large responsibility for people's well-being, including their financial needs. Germany and the United Kingdom, for example, are welfare states. The United States, in many ways, has become one.

The modern welfare state emerged in Germany in the 1880s

under Chancellor Otto von Bismarck when German industrial workers protested poor working and living conditions. Bismarck introduced government programs for sickness insurance, accident insurance, and old-age pensions. Over the next several decades, the welfare state spread to other European nations. Programs expanded to include everything from government-run child care and education to health care and housing assistance.

The idea of the welfare state did not take hold in the United States as soon as it did in Europe. That's because for centuries Europeans had looked to kings and nobility to protect them in times of danger. For many people there, it made sense that modern government should help protect them from problems like unemployment or even sickness.

The United States, on the other hand, was founded on the belief that power concentrated in the hands of government was a threat to liberty. Americans tended to believe that people should take care of themselves, their families, and their neighbors instead of depending on government for basic needs.

That thinking changed during the Great Depression of the 1930s, when millions were thrown out of work. People looked to the government for help, and President Franklin D. Roosevelt introduced programs he called the New Deal to put people back to work and guarantee everyone a standard of living.

The US welfare state grew more in the 1960s with President Lyndon B. Johnson's Great Society programs, which were meant to bring "an end to poverty and racial injustice" and "advance the quality of our American civilization." Liberals wanted to use government to engineer a society that "serves not only the needs of the body and the demands of commerce but the desire for beauty and the hunger for community."[1]

The American welfare state has continued to grow into a vast network of agencies that administer hundreds of programs delivering money, goods, and services to millions of people. Some of the largest and most well-known federal programs are Social Security, which provides monthly checks to the elderly to help with living expenses; Medicare, which covers health care for the elderly; and Medicaid, which provides health care for the poor. In 2010, with the passage of the Affordable Care Act (also known as "Obamacare"), the federal government took control of much of the country's health care system.

Other federal programs include food stamps to help the needy pay for groceries; low-income housing assistance; aid to low-income women and children; unemployment benefits; employment training; free or low-cost school lunches; funding for public education; child care and preschool for poor children; college loans and grants; and payments to low-income people who have jobs.

Those are just a few of the many federal programs. There are also hundreds of agencies and programs run by the states. In the 1980s about a third of Americans lived in a household receiving benefits of some kind from the government. Today about one half of all Americans do.[2] That is stunning growth—but is it good?

How much does the American welfare state cost?

The modern American welfare state is so massive and contains so many programs at the federal and state levels that it's hard for anyone to calculate exactly how much it costs. The bottom line is that it is enormously expensive—its cost dwarfs many countries' entire budgets.

Much of this spending goes to entitlement programs. They're called "entitlements" because people who fall into certain groups are entitled by law to receive benefits. For example, all Americans over the age of 65 who have worked and paid taxes into the system are entitled to Medicare insurance, which pays for health care. Medicare is one of the three most expensive federal entitlement programs. The other two are Medicaid (health care insurance for the poor) and Social Security (retirement income for the elderly).

Over the last half century, entitlement spending has soared. In 1960, it made up well under one-third of federal spending. By 2010, it had grown to about two-thirds. In that year alone, federal, state, and local governments oversaw more than $2.2 trillion of spending on entitlement programs. In order to pay for that amount, government would have to tax every man, woman, and child in the country more than $7,200. And that's for just one year of entitlement spending![3]

"Within living memory, the federal government has become an entitlements machine," observes Nicholas Eberstadt of the American Enterprise Institute. "As a day-to-day operation, it devotes more attention and resources to the public transfer of money, goods and services to individual citizens than to any other objective, spending more than for all other ends combined."[4]

As the American welfare state has grown, government has raised taxes and borrowed more and more money to cover its cost. This spending—particularly on Social Security, Medicare, and Medicaid—is the main reason Americans now face a crushing public debt.

Entitlement spending, along with the cost of paying for our national debt, is on course to swallow every dollar of tax money the federal government collects by 2030.[5]

The United States isn't the only country with this problem. Europe's welfare states have also accumulated massive debts because of unsustainable spending. Their governments, too, will run out of money before long if something does not change.

Has all this spending worked?

Some of it has. Many government efforts—from the Interstate Highway System to programs that help veterans to medical research

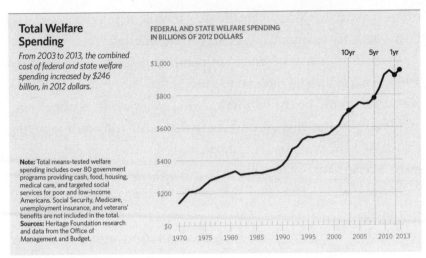

Total Welfare Spending

From 2003 to 2013, the combined cost of federal and state welfare spending increased by $246 billion, in 2012 dollars.

Note: Total means-tested welfare spending includes over 80 government programs providing cash, food, housing, medical care, and targeted social services for poor and low-income Americans. Social Security, Medicare, unemployment insurance, and veterans' benefits are not included in the total.
Sources: Heritage Foundation research and data from the Office of Management and Budget.

FEDERAL AND STATE WELFARE SPENDING
IN BILLIONS OF 2012 DOLLARS

10yr   5yr   1yr

$1,000

$800

$600

$400

$200

$0

1970   1975   1980   1985   1990   1995   2000   2005   2010 2013

Graph courtesy of The Heritage Foundation

that fights disease—have made a positive difference in people's lives. There is no question that in many ways, Americans' tax dollars have done much good.

At the same time, many government programs have not achieved their aims.

Take, for example, the multitude of government programs aimed at fighting poverty. The federal government launched its "War on Poverty" in the 1960s during President Lyndon Johnson's administration. "Our aim is not only to relieve the symptom of poverty, but to cure it and, above all, to prevent it," Johnson declared.[6] In other words, Johnson's goal was to help low-income Americans climb out of poverty and become self-sufficient so they wouldn't need government aid in the future.

Since that time, government has spent more than $20 trillion on programs that provide cash, food, housing, medical care, and other services for the poor. Yet for all that spending, the US Census Bureau reports that the poverty rate has not changed much in the last fifty years. It's stuck at around 15 percent of the population.

Today millions of people are receiving thousands of dollars a year in government benefits, but they still earn very little money on their own.[7]

Aiding the poor is a noble endeavor that we should all want to take part in, but if the aim is to help people climb out of poverty—rather than have them depend on government assistance year after year—then the government's massive spending programs are a terrible failure.

Even programs that have improved people's lives are often poorly designed and run. Social Security and Medicare, for example, have helped millions of Americans but are driving the country further and further into debt. Within two decades, unless something is done, those programs won't have enough money to cover expenses. It will take tens of trillions of dollars to pay out all the Social Security and Medicare benefits the government has promised. No one knows where all that money will come from.[8]

This is a fundamental problem of the modern welfare state. It grows in size and power by promising citizens more and more benefits. But it has often overpromised. It simply does not have the money to pay for it all.

How is an ever-expanding welfare state at odds with conservative principles?

An ever-growing, overreaching welfare state is at odds with conservative principles and common sense in several ways.

First, it is not financially sustainable. Government can't go on borrowing money year after year for entitlement programs it can't afford. At some point, one way or another, someone will have to pay for all the spending. The debt will fall on young people and on future generations. It is morally wrong to cripple them with that burden.

Furthermore, the ever-growing welfare state reduces liberty. The more regulations big government issues, the fewer individual freedoms we have. Big government is sometimes called the "nanny state" because it tries to micromanage people's lives. For example, in the name of looking after citizens' well-being, the federal government has even issued rules saying what sort of food and drinks students can sell at school bake sales.[9]

An overreaching welfare state weakens the American character. That a free people should take responsibility for their own lives is a very American ideal. As the government takes more and more charge of people's well-being, people expect the government to take care of problems for them. That undermines personal responsibility.

It can also undermine the spirit of work. If people don't have to work, many will choose not to. This is human nature. When big government sends the message "You will be taken care of" and then follows that message with years of entitlement benefits, it can erode people's desire to earn their own living. It's no coincidence that as the welfare state has expanded, many people have stopped working.[10]

The more the government does for us, the more we come to rely on it. It creates a sense of dependency on the government while destroying self-reliance. It can even create a sense among people that they are *entitled* to government payouts and services.

President Franklin Roosevelt, who in many ways launched the American welfare state, recognized the dangers of dependency on government. He said that "continued dependence upon relief induces a spiritual and moral disintegration fundamentally destructive to the national fibre. To dole out relief in this way is to administer a narcotic, a subtle destroyer of the human spirit."[11]

Those are good words to ponder as, three quarters of a century later, the welfare state continues to grow.

Do conservatives want to get rid of all government benefit programs?

No. Most conservatives want to change the modern welfare state as we know it—one that is continually growing and taking more power for itself. But they certainly understand that there are people who need help from government programs. They also understand that those people are not just "takers."

Congressman Paul Ryan of Wisconsin tells how he and other policymakers had fallen into the habit of using the phrase "makers and takers" to describe two broad categories of Americans. "Makers" referred to those who pay more taxes than they get back in benefits from the government. "Takers" meant those people who receive more government benefits than they pay in taxes.

One day when Ryan was at the Wisconsin state fair, a man challenged him with the question, "Who, exactly, are the takers?"

"Excuse me?" Ryan asked.

"The makers and the takers," the man said. "I know who the makers are, but who are the takers? Is it the person who lost their job and is on unemployment benefits? Is it the veteran who served in Iraq and gets their medical care through the VA [Veterans Administration]? When you talk about the takers, who exactly do you mean?"

As Ryan listened, he thought, *Holy cow. He's right.* Lumping people into broad categories like "makers and takers" overlooks the real hardships people sometimes face in life. It makes it sound as if people who are struggling are deadbeats. But there are many people who have worked hard, paid their dues, and then for one reason or another fallen on hard times.

Of course, there are real "takers"—people on government assistance who don't really need it, who are abusing the system. There is no doubt about that, and that abuse needs to stop. But as Congressman Ryan points out, there are also millions of Americans who at some point in their lives are in a position of true need, and government can make a difference for them.[12]

Conservatives don't want government to stop helping those people. But they do expect government to operate programs in smart, effective ways that don't waste taxpayer dollars and aren't rife with abuse. They expect government to make a distinction between people who truly need and deserve help and people who are simply looking for a handout.

Conservatives are also realists. They know there are limits to what government can and should do. Government programs that don't get results should be reformed or done away with so resources can be put to work in ways that do get results.

How do conservatives want to help those in need?

Conservatives are against the idea of a welfare state that shepherds people through life with government programs. But they also believe that America should use its vast resources to help those in real need. Here are a few principles that conservatives hold to when it comes to government helping others:

- **Aid should be focused on those who truly need it.**
  Government can and should provide a safety net to help catch those who have fallen on hard times and those who are unable to care for themselves. But a government that keeps promising more and more benefits to more and more people is putting society on a self-destructive course. It will bankrupt the country and end up doing far more harm than good. Instead, we should focus resources on those who need help the most.
- **Government programs must always encourage personal responsibility.** They must never send the message that government can take care of all needs or protect from

all hardship and misfortune in life. Robert Doar, former commissioner of New York City's principal social services agency, put it this way: "The minute [a welfare] applicant believes that government will solve all of her problems, she loses. Accepting responsibility for one's own future is the vital first step to moving up."[13]

Doar and his colleagues applied conservative principles to welfare reform in New York City, and the results were impressive. The number of people on welfare dropped by hundreds of thousands, former welfare recipients went to work, and child poverty levels shrank.

- **Government benefits should not be designed to last forever.** Some programs, such as those that help the elderly or the permanently disabled, must provide long-term help. But generally speaking, programs should be designed to get those in need back on their feet and off government assistance as quickly as possible. When people begin to think of the government as a permanent source of income, it leaves them in a state of dependency.

- **When appropriate, programs should require people to work.** This applies, in particular, to welfare programs for low-income people. One of the best ways to get and keep people off welfare is to require them to work full-time in return for aid. Full-time work is also the best way for people to climb out of poverty.[14]

In 1996, Congress passed legislation reforming a welfare program that provides aid to poor single mothers. The legislation required aid recipients to get full-time work. Many "experts" predicted disaster. They said that welfare mothers could not work and that the change would throw a million more children into poverty. In fact, the opposite happened.

More than a million single mothers found jobs, and poverty levels dropped.[15] More reform like that needs to happen.

- **We must do everything we can to strengthen families.** The decline of the two-parent family is a major cause of poverty in this country. The scholar Lawrence Mead writes, "Poor families typically arise when parents have children without marrying and then do not work regularly to support them. Usually, the father disappears without paying child support, often due to failure to work."[16] The widespread birth of children to unwed mothers has become a national tragedy. Strong, two-parent families are critical for fighting poverty.

Government should not be the first place people look to for help. Conservatives believe it should be a last resort. That belief brings with it a responsibility to step up and help those in need with personal action and giving. In other words, we shouldn't wait for government to help others. We should do it ourselves—through churches, temples, neighborhood associations, charities, civic clubs, or volunteer groups. The best kind of help is given with our own hands.

TAXES *and* SPENDING

On a cold, damp December night in 1773, a few dozen colonists wearing old clothes and blacked faces tramped through the streets of Boston toward three ships tied up at Griffin's Wharf. The Mohawks, as they called themselves, clambered aboard the *Dartmouth*, the *Eleanor*, and the *Beaver* and began hoisting chests of tea from the vessels' holds onto the decks. They carried 342 chests to the rails, split them open, and dumped the tea into Boston Harbor.

The late-night raid was a protest over a tea tax. The Americans were angry that England was taxing them even though they had no representatives in Parliament. To the protestors, taxes and tea had become symbols of British oppression. "No taxation without representation!" sounded up and down the colonies.

In less than three hours, the Boston Tea Party was over. Their work done, the Mohawks swept the ships' decks, bid the crews farewell, and marched into the night whistling "Yankee Doodle." King

George III was outraged at the act of defiance. "We must master them or totally leave them alone!" he declared. His colonies were on the road to revolution.

To this day, taxes remain a touchy subject in America, for all kinds of reasons. They represent one of the major divides between conservatives and liberals. Generally speaking, liberals are apt to favor raising taxes so the government can spend more money. Conservatives, on the other hand, favor lower taxes and less government spending. They believe high taxes and spending can sink the economy and end up hurting everyone.

That's the view of the modern-day Tea Party movement. It takes its name from that long-ago night in Boston. The mainstream media like to paint the Tea Party as extremist. But its message is no less extreme than the patriots' in 1773—and in fact makes much common sense.

Are taxes good or bad?

Most taxpayers would probably call them a necessary evil. We must pay taxes to have a functioning government. Justice Oliver Wendell Holmes put it this way more than a hundred years ago: "Taxes are what we pay for civilized society."[1]

So taxes in general are necessary. But in some cases, they can be harmful.

High taxes are bad because they take money out of the hands of people and businesses that would otherwise be using it to buy things, make things, provide services, and hire workers—in other words, all the activities required to make the economy go.

High taxes also hurt individual freedom. The more the government takes in taxes, the more control it has, and the less freedom you have to use that money the way you want. The Greek philosopher Aristotle pointed out centuries ago that one way ancient tyrants controlled people was to "multiply taxes."[2]

Taxes are bad when the government wastes them. Unfortunately, this happens all the time. For example, the government wastes millions of tax dollars sending food stamps to people who are dead or not entitled to receive them. It has wasted billions subsidizing corporations, from big agriculture companies to green-energy start-ups to defense contractors. It has wasted billions more on duplicative government programs and computer systems.[3]

Taxes are also harmful when they get so complicated that most people can't understand them. That creates confusion and frustration. US income tax laws have become so complex, it takes seventy-four thousand pages to explain them.[4] Every year millions of people have to hire accountants just to figure out how much they might owe.

Albert Einstein once remarked that "the hardest thing in the world to understand is income taxes." When taxes are more complicated than the theory of relativity is to Einstein, something is wrong.

Where does all the money go?

"A billion here, a billion there, pretty soon you're talking real money." The late senator Everett Dirksen of Illinois reportedly uttered that line. It pretty much sums up the way spending goes in Washington, DC.

The nearby chart breaks down federal spending in 2014. In that year, Americans paid about $3 trillion in federal taxes and $1.5 trillion in state taxes.[5] Keep in mind that the federal government actually spends much more than it receives in taxes. In 2014, it borrowed fourteen cents out of every dollar it spent.[6]

Most of the federal budget goes to programs that provide benefits to people. Medicare (health care insurance for the elderly), Medicaid (health care insurance for the poor), and Social Security (retirement income for the elderly) are the three largest government benefit programs. Altogether, these major benefit programs account for about five out of every ten dollars the federal government spends.

Graph courtesy of The Heritage Foundation

These programs are growing and taking over more of the federal budget every year. If nothing changes, benefit programs and interest paid on the national debt will take over the entire federal budget within a generation.[7] There will be no money left for vital government functions such as providing for national defense, running the court system, or keeping ambassadors overseas. There will not even be enough money left over to collect taxes.

How do high taxes hurt people?

High income taxes can hurt people by hurting the economy. Here's how it works.

When the government takes more from people in taxes, they have less money in their pockets to buy things. That means less business for the makers and sellers of those products. That slows the economy down, which can throw people out of work and make it harder to find good jobs. (The government puts tax money to work in the economy, but government spending is less productive and efficient than private-sector spending.)

High taxes take money out of the hands of entrepreneurs and other businesspeople. That's less money to launch new companies, buy inventory, and hire workers. All of that slows the economy.

High income taxes can also discourage work. That's simply human nature. If you know that the government is going to take one quarter of your income, you might be inclined to hustle and make as much as you can. But if the government starts taking half of your income or more, you might very well ask yourself, "What's the point of working hard if I'm not going to be able to keep much of what I make?"

Finally, high taxes can keep people from saving. Every dollar that goes to the government is one less dollar someone has to put into a retirement account or invest in the stock market.

Lower taxes, on the other hand, can have the opposite effect. Tax cuts can make the economy stronger. The lower the tax rate, the more incentive people have to work, start a business, expand a company, make a new product, or create jobs. And the more freedom they have to use the money they make as they see fit, whether buying things, investing, or saving.

Every year, the Tax Foundation calculates Tax Freedom Day, the day when the United States as a whole has earned enough money to pay its tax bill. It's a handy way to understand how much of the nation's income goes to taxes.

In 2015, Tax Freedom Day came on April 24. For the first 113 days of the year—nearly a third of the calendar—America was working for the government, so to speak. Beginning April 24, we got to work for ourselves and our families.[8]

Liberals who want to raise taxes should answer the question, exactly how much of the year should we have to work for the government?

Don't higher taxes bring in more money for the government?

Not necessarily. To understand the full story on high taxes, you have to know about something called the Laffer Curve. The concept is named after Arthur Laffer, a well-known American economist.

The Laffer Curve illustrates an important point that modern-day economists have come to learn about taxes. As the graph below shows, when tax rates are low, raising them can bring in more revenue to the government.

At some point, however, if the government raises taxes too much, those high taxes will start to be a drag on the economy for the reasons explained above. As the economy slows down, people and businesses make less money. That means there is less income and profit for the government to tax.

As a result, tax revenues for the government begin to drop—even though the government is raising the tax rate. The more the government raises tax rates, the more the economy slows, and the less tax revenue the government receives.

Economists disagree about the exact point at which high tax rates

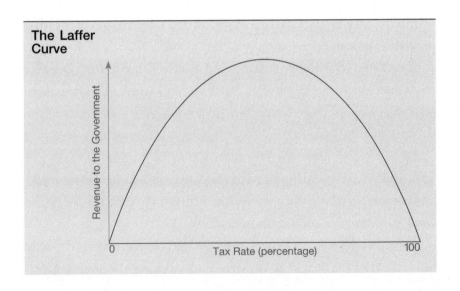

The Laffer Curve

Revenue to the Government

0   Tax Rate (percentage)   100

begin to send tax revenues down. Much depends on the kind of tax, the state of the economy, and other factors.

The bottom line is that raising tax rates too much can actually decrease tax money coming to the government. This happened, for example, during the Great Depression of the 1930s. The government raised taxes on imported goods with a law known as the Smoot-Hawley Tariff, but revenues from those taxes went down.

For a good online explanation of the Laffer Curve and how it works, visit the Prager University website (www.prageruniversity.com) and watch the economics video called "Lower Taxes, Higher Revenue."

Why can't rich people pay all the taxes?

First, let's see what would happen if we asked super-rich people to pay all the taxes—multibillionaires like Bill Gates (founder of Microsoft), Warren Buffett (the country's most famous investor), and Larry Page and Sergey Brin (founders of Google).

In 2014, Bill Gates was worth around $80 billion. The federal government spent about $3.5 trillion that year.[9] That means the government could seize all of Bill Gates's wealth and would get only *one forty-fourth* of the money needed to cover its expenses for that year. It would still need to find forty-three other people about as rich as Bill Gates and take all of their wealth to pay for just one year of spending. The problem is that there are very few people anywhere near as rich as Bill Gates.

You can see where this is going. The government would very quickly eat up all the fortunes it could find. There just aren't enough billionaires to cover the federal government's spending year after year. And we haven't even taken into account the spending of state and local governments.

What about the people who aren't super rich but still make a lot of money? What if the government demanded that they pay all the taxes?

In fact, they already do pay a huge portion of the nation's annual tax bill. Just 5 percent of all taxpayers make over $200,000 a year, but that top 5 percent pays about 70 percent of all federal income taxes paid by the American people.[10]

The Bible tells us that of those to whom much is given, much is asked.[11] That's an important truth to remember. But it's also important to remember, perhaps with some gratitude, that high earners do carry a big part of the tax burden in this country. Much is asked of them, and they do give.

Why can't we just tax corporations more?

The United States already has a corporate tax rate of nearly 40 percent, including federal, state, and local taxes. That's one of the highest corporate tax rates among developed countries.[12] Companies can use tax breaks to lower their rates, but generally speaking, they still pay higher taxes here than in many other nations.

When government raises taxes on a corporation, that company has to find a way to cover the additional cost of doing business. One way is to raise the price of its product or service, passing the cost along to the consumer, which means that you and I are the ones who really end up paying the tax.

Corporations might also decide to relocate to states or countries with lower taxes. In this age of global markets and instant communication, many companies can operate from wherever it makes good economic sense to be. If you were the head of a corporation, would you want to be in a place that hit your company with high taxes if you could help it? Probably not.

In the view of many conservatives and even some liberals, the best strategy is to lower corporate tax rates. That attracts corporations looking for good business climates. The more companies a state or country can attract, the more jobs are available to people and the more taxes government can collect.

It's important to recognize the source of the revenues that keep government running. It's the private sector—companies large and small. When government gets too greedy for those revenues, it can drive companies away and lose its tax base.

An Aesop fable we all learned as children applies here. A man and his wife had the good fortune to possess a goose that laid a golden egg every day. As lucky as they were, they wanted even more. They imagined the goose must be made of gold inside, and they decided to kill the goose to get it. But when the man sliced into the bird, he discovered that it was just like any other. Their goose was dead, and they got no more gold.

Should taxes be used to redistribute wealth?

The United States has a progressive income tax system. That means people who earn more money pay a greater percentage of their income in taxes to fund government programs, including programs for the needy. It's a redistribution of wealth from those with more to those with less.

As long as the system helps those truly in need within reasonable limits, most Americans are fine with it. But if "redistributing wealth" really means "I'm taking money from you because it's not fair that you have more than I do," then many people have a big problem with it.

Liberals often accuse wealthy Americans of not paying their "fair share" and call for taxing them more. Here are a few facts and questions to think about when you hear such talk.

The top federal tax rate on people who earn a lot of money is about 40 percent. (Like all taxpayers, they can use tax breaks to lower their federal taxes, but they still face other taxes, such as state and local taxes, taxes on investments, and self-employment taxes.) How much more of their income is it "fair" to take? Sixty percent? Eighty percent? What is a "fair" amount to take from *your* income?

Many government programs are wasteful, ineffective, and out of control when it comes to spending. Is it "fair" for the government to take more money from anyone to pay for such programs?

The top one percent of US taxpayers (the wealthiest) pay about a third of all federal income taxes collected by the government.[13] That means a very small portion of Americans pay a large part of the nation's federal tax bill. So is it "fair" to suggest that people who make a lot of money are not paying their "fair share"? Or is that class warfare?

GOVERNMENT DEBT

Think what you do when you run in debt; you give to another power over your liberty.
If you cannot pay at the time, you will be ashamed to see your creditor; you will be
in fear when you speak to him; you will make poor pitiful sneaking excuses, and, by
degrees, come to lose your veracity, and sink into base, downright lying; for, "The second
vice is lying, the first is running in debt," as Poor Richard says; and again, to the same
purpose, "Lying rides upon Debt's back:" whereas a free-born Englishman ought not to
be ashamed nor afraid to see or speak to any man living. But poverty often deprives a
man of all spirit and virtue. "It is hard for an empty bag to stand upright."
—BENJAMIN FRANKLIN, *The Way to Wealth*, 1758

BENJAMIN FRANKLIN WOULD be horrified at the situation the United States has let itself get into. For years, the federal government has been spending more money than it has. It has piled up an enormous mountain of debt—$18 trillion and rising as of 2015.

That's roughly $60,000 of debt for each man, woman, and child in this country. That doesn't even include debts that state and local governments have racked up.[1]

If you want to see how fast the debt is mounting, go to the US National Debt Clock website (www.usdebtclock.org) and take a look. You won't like what you see.

Here is the bottom line: the United States is on the road to serious financial problems, perhaps even financial catastrophe. If you are a young American, you should be particularly alarmed. Unless something is done soon, a debt this size may crush your chances for a prosperous future.

What's causing so much national debt?

One word: spending. Uncle Sam is like a man with a credit card on a shopping spree. He keeps charging more and more things, but he doesn't have the money to pay for them.

Almost every year during the last few decades, the federal government has spent more money than it gets in taxes. The difference between its expenditures and its tax revenues each year is called the budget deficit. Each year, the government has to borrow money to make up for the deficit and cover all its bills.

The amount the government borrows varies from year to year, depending on the deficit. In 2014, it borrowed fourteen cents out of every dollar spent.[2]

The government borrows money from all sorts of places—foreign countries like China and Japan, banks, mutual fund investors, and state and local governments. It sells bonds to these lenders and promises to pay them back with interest.

But the government doesn't have enough money in any one year to pay back what it owes *and* to keep spending so much. So it keeps borrowing more and more. That means its debt—the total of all the money it owes—keeps going up.

What is the government spending so much money on?

Most of the spending goes toward massive programs that pay out benefits to millions of people. In 2014, about half the federal budget went to Social Security (retirement income for the elderly), Medicare (health care insurance for the elderly), Medicaid (health care insurance for the poor), Obamacare, and other health insurance spending.[3] These programs have been growing rapidly and are expected to keep growing as the country's population ages.

Interest on the debt—the money Uncle Sam pays to lenders every year as the price of borrowing money from them—is another part of the budget that keeps growing. The more we borrow, the more interest we have to pay off. Before too long, if we don't change course, we will be spending a trillion dollars a year just to pay interest on the debt.[4]

What will happen if the debt keeps growing?

Think about what would happen if you kept putting more and more charges onto a credit card. The bigger your debt, the larger your

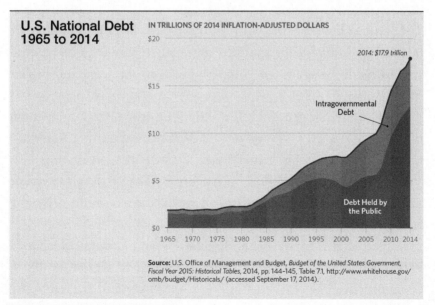

U.S. National Debt 1965 to 2014

IN TRILLIONS OF 2014 INFLATION-ADJUSTED DOLLARS

2014: $17.9 trillion

Intragovernmental Debt

Debt Held by the Public

Source: U.S. Office of Management and Budget, *Budget of the United States Government, Fiscal Year 2015: Historical Tables*, 2014, pp. 144–145, Table 7.1, http://www.whitehouse.gov/omb/budget/Historicals/ (accessed September 17, 2014).

Graph courtesy of The Heritage Foundation

monthly payments to the credit card company. You could spend years struggling to pay off the debt instead of buying things you really needed, such as a house or a car. If you couldn't make your monthly credit card payments, you might even go into bankruptcy.

The circumstances are not identical with governments, but the laws of finance are the same: debts must be paid or bad things happen.

As the United States keeps borrowing money, its interest payments on the debt grow. In fact, interest payments could eventually turn into the largest single expense the government has.[5] We could end up spending more money paying back our creditors than we'll spend on vital government jobs such as maintaining an army to defend ourselves. Meanwhile, our huge payments to countries that have loaned us money, like China, will go to building *their* armies and making *their* nations richer.

As the nation's debt gets out of control, all sorts of bad things can happen. The government may eventually hike taxes to help pay for all its borrowing and spending. Big tax increases would fall mainly on the middle class since it is the largest source of taxable income. That would leave people with less money to buy things and start businesses. A huge debt could force the government to make deep cuts to many programs. It could also lead to inflation and higher interest rates.

All of these things would slow economic growth and weaken job markets, perhaps for a long time. The debt could put the American Dream at risk for rising generations.

In a worst-case scenario, a huge debt could cause the government to start having problems paying all its bills. That could drive the economy into a downward spiral.

If you want to see what happens when a country spends itself into a crisis, read about what happened to Greece in 2010. Government debt reached the breaking point, and the economy went into free fall. Businesses went under. Thousands lost their jobs. The government announced it would have to cut services and raise taxes. People rioted in the streets. Other European nations had to step in and bail Greece out.

Or, closer to home, read about what happened to Detroit, Michigan, in 2013. Years of local government overspending, borrowing, and mismanagement played a major role in driving a once-glittering city into financial ruin and bankruptcy. "That was the whole culture—how do we get what we want and not pay for it until tomorrow and tomorrow and tomorrow?" a former Detroit budget staffer said.[6]

Is debt going to throw the United States into financial ruin tomorrow? No. But twenty or thirty years down the road, it could cause serious economic problems.

That's why young people—students or recent graduates, for example—should be especially alarmed over government debt. If you are young, the burden is going to fall on you. You'll have to pay, one way or another, for all the spending and borrowing that is going on today.

Why does the government keep spending so much money?

There are several reasons. One is a growing country. More people means more for the government to do. Another reason is greater affluence. Wealthy populations tend to expect more government services. Another is changing attitudes. Over time, Americans have voted for bigger and bigger government.

Some programs—entitlements such as Social Security and Medicare—are by law on autopilot to cost more with time. As the population grows and ages, these programs pay out more benefits every year.

Much of the spending is the result of government's natural tendency to expand. Here is a truth about modern American democracy that conservatives have learned over the years: once a government program gets going, it is extremely difficult to end it.

In fact, the opposite almost always happens. Government programs tend to keep growing, taking on lives of their own and costing more every year. Each program gains a constituency of voters who benefit from it and howl when anyone suggests cutting back. They pressure Congress to get more funding, not less.

The debt problem grows every year, but a crisis is still years away. It's much easier for lawmakers to put off fixing things than to face the pain of cutting back. Like the man addicted to his credit card, the government keeps overspending even though it realizes it's only making things worse.

Here's another truth that applies to modern American government: it's easy to spend other people's money. Many lawmakers go to Washington because they want to use government to fix problems and to improve the country. It doesn't take long for them to start thinking, *Just a few million dollars here or a few billion dollars over there would help things*. That money doesn't come out of their own pockets, of course. That makes it so much easier to vote for big government programs. So the spending and borrowing goes on.

Margaret Thatcher, a great British prime minister in the latter part of the twentieth century, used to say that the problem with socialism is you eventually run out of other people's money. The same could be said of a government with debt spiraling out of control. The day will come when there is no more money to borrow.

How do we bring our debt problem under control?

Conservatives believe that the best way out of debt is to rein in government spending, make serious reforms to government programs, and use the power of free enterprise to grow the nation's economy.

When the economy grows, people and businesses make more

money, which means the government collects more tax revenue. It can use that new revenue to pay off debt.

Meanwhile, the federal government will have to break its bad habit of spending so much. In particular, it will have to reform popular entitlement programs that are bankrupting the country, including Social Security, Medicare, and Medicaid.

Restraining the growth of government spending is a hard choice for politicians to make. But not long ago, Americans discovered that it is, in fact, possible to trim the government's budget. In 2013, Congress cut $85 billion in spending. It was a tiny portion of the federal budget, but liberals still warned of dire consequences: over a million lost jobs, disruptions in air travel, increased risks of wildfires, closed housing projects, and hundreds of thousands of women and children thrown out of aid programs, to name a few predictions.[7]

None of the doomsday warnings came true. The government managed to tighten its belt, and the country went on. In fact, the budget cuts led to only one government job being lost![8]

As the debt increases, many liberals will argue that raising tax rates is the key to paying it off. But thinking that we can tax our way out of debt is a mistake. Higher taxes will place a heavier burden on future generations. They could siphon money away from the private sector and stymie the economy.

If you had a credit card problem and sat down with a credit counselor, she would not say, "Well, you just need to go out and get more money so you can keep spending." The first thing she would say is "Stop spending so much!"

Common sense is a good guide here. If we can use the powerful American economy to bring more revenue to the government and bring the government's spending down to sensible levels, we can stabilize the nation's finances. That will make the future for young Americans much brighter.

Part 3

INDIVIDUAL LIBERTY

INDIVIDUAL LIBERTY

Here are some of the most important words ever written in America:

Amendment I
Congress shall make no law respecting an establishment of religion, or prohibiting the free exercise thereof; or abridging the freedom of speech, or of the press; or the right of the people peaceably to assemble, and to petition the Government for a redress of grievances.

Amendment II
A well regulated Militia, being necessary to the security of a free State, the right of the people to keep and bear Arms, shall not be infringed.

Amendment IV

The right of the people to be secure in their persons, houses, papers, and effects, against unreasonable searches and seizures, shall not be violated. . . .

Recognize them? They're part of the Bill of Rights, the first ten amendments to the Constitution. The founders wrote them to ensure that government doesn't trample individuals' rights and liberties, such as freedom of speech and freedom of religion.

We often take such liberty for granted. It's easy to think, *Of course I'm free to say what I think and to worship however I want.*

That's a mistake, because the liberties we Americans enjoy are fragile blessings. Much of the world does not have such freedom. It always needs protecting. *Always.* "Eternal vigilance is the price of liberty," an old saying goes. It's absolutely true.

James Madison and the other authors of the Bill of Rights knew that government must protect individuals' liberties. But they also understood that the natural tendency of government to accumulate power can erode individual liberty.

"I believe there are more instances of the abridgment of the freedom of the people by gradual and silent encroachments of those in power, than by violent and sudden usurpations," Madison warned.[1] In other words, beware of government slowly chipping away at your liberty. The bigger government gets—as it has in the last several decades—the greater the temptation for government officials to restrict freedom.

It's very important to remember that liberty walks hand in hand with responsibility. American freedom rests on the idea that most people are capable of being responsible for their own affairs and should be. Every time we don't take responsibility for our own affairs and instead place that responsibility in government's hands, we give up some of our freedom.

This chapter examines some issues that involve your liberties as an American citizen. As you think about them, you might want to ask yourself, *What sort of vigilance does liberty need today? And what sort of responsibilities come with my liberty?*

Is the left tolerant of free speech?

Liberals like to think of themselves as tolerant, but there are a lot of people on the left who seem to think it's okay to silence those who don't agree with them. They're especially keen on excluding conservative viewpoints. Here are a few examples:

- During President Barack Obama's administration, officials at the Internal Revenue Service tried to muzzle dozens of groups supporting conservative causes by denying or slowing down their requests for tax-exempt status. The effort was led by a supporter of President Obama, who wrote that conservatives pose a bigger threat than "alien teRrorists [sic]."[2]
- Dismayed by surveys showing that the majority of TV meteorologists don't buy the idea of human-caused global warming, climate change activists have launched a campaign to force them to change their views or get them off the air. "These climate denier meteorologists are betraying the public's trust and distorting America's airwaves," one liberal publication reported.[3]
- In 2012 liberal government officials in Chicago, Boston, and other cities threatened to keep fast-food chain Chick-fil-A out of their communities after company CEO Dan Cathy stated his belief that marriage should be between a man and a woman. "Chick-fil-A values are not Chicago values," the mayor of Chicago explained.[4]

- At many universities, liberal students and professors try their best to keep people they disagree with from speaking on campus. One student at Swarthmore College put it this way after a visit by Princeton professor Robert George: "I don't think we should be tolerating [George's] conservative views because that dominant culture embeds these deep inequalities in our society."[5]
- In 2014 Brandeis University in Massachusetts canceled an invitation to Ayaan Hirsi Ali to receive an honorary degree. Hirsi Ali is a Somali-born feminist known as a crusader for women's rights, especially in Muslim societies. Brandeis withdrew its invitation because she had made statements deemed critical of Islam.[6]
- In 2014 Harvard's student newspaper, the *Crimson*, carried a column that proposed replacing academic freedom with "a more rigorous standard: one of 'academic justice.' When an academic community observes research promoting or justifying oppression, it should ensure that this research does not continue." Of course, liberals like that student columnist would hold "the power to enforce academic justice" by deciding what sort of research should or should not continue.[7]

To be fair, some liberals are unhappy with efforts to shut down debate. Yet despite claims of being open minded, far too many on the left have become intolerant of opposing viewpoints.

How does the Affordable Care Act affect individual liberty?

The Affordable Care Act (also known as "Obamacare") is a massive law passed by Democrats in Congress and signed by President Obama in 2010 with the aim of lowering health care costs and getting more people covered by health insurance. Conservatives don't like the law for several reasons. One main objection is that it infringes on people's liberty.

Under Obamacare, the government has assumed control over a big chunk of the nation's health care system. It sets requirements about buying health insurance, and it taxes people if they don't buy insurance to the government's liking. It dictates rules about the policies that insurance companies offer and the plans that businesses offer their employees.

For many conservatives, the issue boils down to this question: How much power should the government have over our health care, one of the most personal aspects of our lives? Because one thing is for certain: the more control the government has, the less freedom we have.

When government calls the shots about health care, it controls decisions about our bodies. That's a tremendous amount of power for government to have, especially since bureaucracies tend to treat people as numbers rather than individuals.

There are other reasons conservatives object to Obamacare, including the dishonest way that President Obama and other liberals sold it to the American people. They said that if people liked their doctor and health care plan, they'd be able to keep them. Many Americans have discovered that isn't true. One of the architects of Obamacare was caught on video boasting that the public had been misled about the law and that "the stupidity of the American voter . . . was really, really critical for the thing to pass."[8]

Obamacare has spawned thousands of pages of regulations, and more are being written. The system is so complex, hardly anyone really understands it. As this book was being written, the US Supreme Court was scheduled to rule on a legal challenge that could end up crippling the entire law.

No one knows how much Obamacare will end up costing taxpayers, but if history is any guide, you can bet it will be much more than projected. In short, it shows all the signs of a bloated, bureaucracy-ridden, budget-busting government program that delivers mediocre results at best.

Many liberals view Obamacare as a step toward what they really want: a socialized health care system completely run by the government. That's something conservatives adamantly oppose. People in countries with government-run health care often face a tangled bureaucracy, limited choices, and long waits for surgery and other needed procedures.

Supporters of Obamacare claim the law does nothing to infringe on anyone's freedom. So here are a couple of additional questions to think about.

Are thousands and thousands of pages of federal health care regulations likely to increase or decrease liberty? And is expanding federal bureaucracy even more really going to do much for your health?

Is the right to have a gun an outdated notion we need to scrap?

No. The founders knew what they were doing when they wrote the Second Amendment, which ensures "the right of the people to keep and bear Arms." That right is important to this day.

When they wrote the Constitution and Bill of Rights, the founders had just finished winning their liberty. They knew from experience that sometimes people have to fight for their rights, their safety, and their lives.

"But the world is a different place now," someone might say. "We're not in a fight with a king for our freedom. Wouldn't it be better to pass a law making it illegal to own guns? That would make the country a much safer place."

The problem with laws that prohibit people from owning firearms is that law-abiding people are the only ones who will consistently obey them. Criminals won't—breaking laws, after all, is what criminals do.

That means criminals would have guns, and honest citizens wouldn't. If you were a criminal, would you be more inclined to break into a home if you knew the people living there had no way to defend themselves? Or if you knew they might have a gun to stop you?

"Well, let's try some laws that make it hard for people to have guns and see how they work," someone might reply. In fact, those kinds of gun control laws have been tried in several different parts of the country. There's no evidence that they reduce crime. Some places with strict gun control laws have higher violent crime rates than areas with fewer gun restrictions.[9]

Here's the critical point that many on the left fail to grasp. Guns themselves are neither good nor bad. People use them for good or bad purposes. Laws keeping guns out of good people's hands are not going to stop bad people from getting and using guns. They only leave the good people more vulnerable.

The problem is not guns themselves. The problem is criminal and antisocial behavior. That's why conservatives favor tough laws that throw the book at people who use guns in crimes. Criminals should know that when they reach for a gun, they're reaching for a long time in prison.

None of this is to say that people should be able to have any kind of gun or weapon anytime they want. Second Amendment rights, like others, are not unlimited. For example, there is no constitutional right to take a gun into a school or to own a nuclear warhead.

Obviously, reasonable laws are in order. For example, many Americans believe it makes sense to require background checks before people buy guns to keep criminals and people who are mentally ill from purchasing them.

This is an example of individual liberty coming with great individual responsibility. The freedom to own guns works only when people take care in how they use them. Conservatives trust that most people will use guns in a responsible manner—which in fact they do.

"Let's get rid of guns" isn't a realistic or constitutional solution. Better to focus efforts on stopping and punishing people who use guns to do bad things.

Is freedom of religion alive and well in the United States?

Overall, the United States does a good job of getting this liberty right. Americans are among the most tolerant and respectful people in the world when it comes to matters of religion. We're free to worship God (or to not worship) according to our different faiths, just as the founders envisioned.

Still, freedom of religion can't be taken for granted. Throughout history, it's been one of the hardest liberties for people to keep.

One potential threat comes from religion itself, in the form of religious extremism, the kind of religion that forces itself on people and says, "Worship and live this way or else."

Radical Islam is such a threat. For example, members of the Islamic State in Iraq and Syria (ISIS) will spill as much blood as necessary to spread their caliphate (a Muslim state ruled by the successor of Muhammad). ISIS members believe that "infidels" deserve beheading and blowing up. "Our message to the entire world is that we are the soldiers of the Caliphate state and we are coming," they've announced.[10]

If we want to make sure that kind of extremism stays outside our borders, the United States has to keep its defenses up and its tradition of religious liberty strong. It also has to safeguard another liberty: free speech in the criticism of extreme religious views. People must feel free to speak up against dangerous religious thought.

A second potential threat against liberty is very different. It does not occur on a regular basis in the United States, but we have to be vigilant about it. It's the threat of government exerting its power and, in the process, trampling on religious liberty.

In 2014, for example, the city of Houston, Texas, issued subpoenas demanding that pastors of five churches turn over any sermons they had given about homosexuality. The demand was a blatant attempt to intimidate religious groups opposed to a city law allowing men dressed as women to use ladies' restrooms and vice versa. "If the 5 pastors used pulpits for politics, their sermons are fair game," the mayor of Houston tweeted.[11] The city later backed down and withdrew the subpoenas after a public outcry.

Is that the kind of country you want to live in—one where government officials bully ministers into handing over sermons and "teachings on sexuality and gender identity" because they don't like their religious beliefs?

Even in America, freedom of religion always needs safeguarding. It's no accident it comes first on the list in the Bill of Rights.

Are US spy agencies a threat to our own liberty?

Technology advances have changed the nature of the spy business in recent years, and with those changes have come new concerns about individual liberties.

The National Security Agency (NSA) has been a focus of controversy. It's a super-secret intelligence agency that monitors and collects data on billions of communications around the globe every day—cell phone calls, e-mails, Facebook chats, Internet traffic. Since the NSA works behind closed doors, few people know exactly what kind of information it collects or how it operates.

Why collect such a massive amount of data? The NSA's job is to track down terrorists and others who want to do the United States harm. Intelligence officials are basically looking for needles in a giant haystack. They use computer programs to "data mine" those billions of communications, searching for clues about where the bad guys are and what they're up to.

Conservatives are of two different minds about this issue. Those sympathetic to a libertarian position, as well as those upset by government overstepping its bounds so often in recent years, are likely to say, "Hold on. Giving government power to scoop up so much information in secret is asking for trouble. How do we know what they're going to do with it?"

They have a good point. The more power government assumes, the greater the chances that someone may abuse that power—for example, by using information against political opponents. When government operates in secrecy, it's hard if not impossible to know when it's misusing power until it's too late.

The NSA reportedly collects data on practically all phone calls made in the United States (though not what's said in those conversations). That kind of broad surveillance, critics say, threatens people's privacy and violates the Fourth Amendment, which is supposed to protect citizens from "unreasonable searches."

Conservatives who focus on national defense view it a bit differently. They say, "Look, we don't really like it either, but we're in a war with terrorists. When you're in a war, government has to do what's necessary to keep us safe, and sometimes government has to do it in secret." That's a good point too.

Supporters of the NSA's programs remind us that the first duty of government is to protect citizens and that we need to use every tool at our disposal to track down terrorists. The NSA targets foreign suspects, not US citizens. It operates under rules designed to safeguard Americans' privacy and collects information with warrants issued by a special court.

People have mixed feelings about this issue. We want our privacy, but we also want to be safe. For many, it comes down to this question: How much do we trust our own government? Unfortunately, confidence in government is pretty low these days. Nevertheless, given the threats toward our national security and how hard it is to stop terrorists, on balance the NSA program makes sense.

THE RULE *of* LAW

ONE OF THE WORST ABUSES OF power in recent American history targeted conservatives. Beginning in 2010, the Internal Revenue Service—the agency in charge of enforcing tax law—zeroed in on groups advocating for conservative issues.

Tea Party groups and other conservative organizations were applying for tax-exempt status. The IRS barraged them with demands for information, including names of donors, copies of Facebook posts, and what books members were reading. At least one pro-life group was instructed to provide details about prayer meetings. The demands for information dragged on. Meanwhile, very few liberal groups were scrutinized.[1]

In 2013, when the IRS's activities became public, a political firestorm erupted. Republicans in Congress demanded that the agency explain its actions, but officials stonewalled. After months of promising to turn over e-mail records, the IRS informed Congress that they had been destroyed. A Treasury Department investigation later found thousands of the "missing" records. E-mails gathered from other sources showed that one top IRS official had referred to conservatives as "—holes" and "crazies."[2]

As of this writing, an investigation into the scandal was still ongoing. President Barack Obama declared that there was "not even a smidgen of corruption" in the IRS's actions.[3]

In fact, there is plenty of evidence of corruption. The IRS, one of the most powerful and intimidating government agencies, conducted a bureaucratic assault on conservatives because officials did not like their political views. Such action is a betrayal of democracy. And it strikes at one of this country's bedrock principles—the rule of law.

What does the "rule of law" mean?

The rule of law is the principle that law should govern a nation, not the wishes of kings, dictators, or government officials. Its opposite is the "rule of men." That's when rulers set themselves above the law and issue commands as they see fit, often in their own interests, not in the interests of the people.

When well-written laws are the authority of the land, people can expect their government to operate in fair, predictable ways. On the other hand, when officials have the power to make up and change rules as they go along, anything can happen. Freedom is usually the first casualty. Individual liberty can't survive for long when government has unrestrained power to say, "Do this" and "Don't do that."

Likewise, liberty suffers when people lose respect for the law. A community or country where people don't obey the law is a place where no one is free to feel safe, own property, or live without their rights being violated.

Abraham Lincoln knew that reverence for the law is crucial in a free nation. "Let every American, every lover of liberty, every well wisher to his posterity, swear by the blood of the Revolution, never to violate in the least particular, the laws of the country; and never to tolerate their violation by others," he wrote. "Let every man remember that to violate the law, is to trample on the blood of his father, and to tear the character of his own, and his children's liberty."[4]

The rule of law is a big reason that millions of people around the world want to live in or do business in the United States. They believe they can count on the United States being a place where most people obey the law, where property rights are respected, and where authorities help protect against lawbreakers.

When government abuses its power—as it did in the IRS scandal—it severely damages the rule of law. It breeds cynicism and destroys confidence in government. It leaves people asking themselves, *If government breaks the rules, why shouldn't I?*

Do big government bureaucracies weaken the rule of law?

They certainly can. Government bureaucracies often give us rule by decree, not rule of law. Here's how it works.

We learn in school that the Constitution divides the federal government into three main branches: the legislative branch writes the law, the executive branch enforces the law, and the judicial branch interprets the law. That is how our federal government is supposed to work.

The truth is that much of government no longer follows that plan. Instead, Congress often passes vague laws and leaves it to bureaucracies such as the Environmental Protection Agency and the Department of Health and Human Services to come up with the specifics. Unelected government officials finish writing the laws through regulations. Not only do they write the regulations, but the same bureaucracies enforce their regulations, impose fines, and act as judges when disputes over the regulations come up.

For example, Congress may pass a law saying that companies can't engage in unfair trade practices, but it leaves it up to the Federal Trade Commission to define "unfair," decide if businesses are being unfair, and issue fines as it sees fit. Likewise, the US Fish and Wildlife Service can tell landowners what they can and can't do with their land if it decides it might affect a species the agency has defined as threatened or endangered.[5]

Government agencies that become lawgiver, police officer, judge, and jury are not what the founders had in mind when they designed a government with a separation of powers. As James Madison wrote, the "accumulation of all powers, legislative, executive, and judiciary, in the same hands . . . may justly be pronounced the very definition of tyranny."[6]

Federal regulators hold enormous power over the decisions people and businesses make. They can shut down businesses, ban ingredients from food, and tell people what kind of health insurance they can buy.

Many bureaucrats lean to the left politically. They like the idea of using government to fashion society to their way of thinking, and they write regulations to exert more control. Some of them think that, just because they live in Washington, DC, they know better than the rest of the country. They don't.

Obviously, some regulations are necessary. But when unelected officials get to dictate how we should live based on how *they* think the world should be, we no longer live under the rule of law. We live by government decree.

Why do conservatives hold police officers in high regard?

Conservatives view police officers as upholders of the rule of law. They are the "thin blue line" that stands between the public and criminals—between the lawful and the unlawful.

Government's first responsibility is to provide for the security of citizens. Without law and order, society falls into chaos. But law and order can't exist without someone to enforce the law. That's where the police come in.

Respect for law enforcement authority is necessary in any civilized society. When that respect erodes, lawlessness is sure to follow.

Sometimes the police make mistakes, including tragic mistakes like shooting innocent people. And not all police officers are good. Like any group of human beings, there are some who are irresponsible and even corrupt. When police officers do wrong, they need to be called out and, if appropriate, prosecuted.

It's also true that America's history includes times when police forces in some communities have mistreated and even brutalized minorities. Honesty requires us all to recognize that. That history has left a strained relationship between citizens and the police in some places.

But it's important to recognize that in this country today, you can almost always count on police officers to stand for right against wrong. They stand for our safety, our rights, and our freedom. Most of them are people motivated by a genuine desire to serve and protect. Many put their lives on the line every day doing just that.

It's also important to understand that our poorest neighborhoods, including ones in our inner cities, need the police most of all. The vast majority of those neighborhoods' residents are decent, law-abiding citizens. Many are scared to death of the drug dealers and other criminals on their streets. They want more, not less, police protection.

Here's something to think about. Imagine for a minute that you are in real trouble—someone bad is threatening your life or destroying your property. Who do you want there right beside you, right away, to save you from harm? If you're like most Americans, you want a cop.

We call on the police when we're in desperate trouble because they're the good guys, the ones who stand for the rule of law.

What is "judicial activism"?

One of this book's coauthors once heard a student ask a New Hampshire judge, "Do judges make law?" The judge admitted, "Yep, I've made some myself."

That's not the way it's supposed to be. Elected legislators, not judges, are supposed to write the laws. But the truth is that courts "make law" all the time.

It's called judicial activism, and it happens when judges let their personal or political views guide their decisions rather than going by what the law says. When issuing an opinion, the judge actively reshapes the law to suit his or her idea of what it should say. Sometimes judicial activism is called "legislating from the bench."

The big problem with judicial activism is that it undermines the rule of law. In place of representative democracy, judges impose their own beliefs on people.

We like to think of judges as unbiased individuals who apply strict logic to the questions before them. But they are human beings like the rest of us, and often their own values and political opinions get mixed into their rulings. Presidents know this. That's why they're likely to appoint federal judges who share their own philosophical and political beliefs.

Many liberal judges believe in the concept of a "living Constitution." They think that as the world changes, courts should reinterpret the Constitution to give it new meanings with new principles to fit the times. The concept of a living Constitution gives activist judges a freer hand to interpret laws according to how they see things and to change laws they don't like.

Roe v. Wade, a 1973 United States Supreme Court case, is a famous example of judicial activism. In that case, the court ruled that women have a fundamental right to abortion under the Constitution. Yet there is nothing at all in the Constitution about a right to abortion. The Supreme Court simply invented it.

As Justice Byron White wrote in a dissenting opinion, "I find nothing in the language or history of the Constitution to support the Court's judgment. The Court simply fashions and announces a new constitutional right for pregnant mothers." Justice White called the Supreme Court's action "an exercise of raw judicial power."[7]

What is "judicial restraint"?

Conservatives believe that judges should use "judicial restraint" in interpreting law. That is, they should restrain themselves from using their rulings to rewrite laws. Instead, they should base their decisions on what the Constitution and the laws say, not what judges think they *should* say.

If laws are bad, or if they need changing in some way, the best place to fix them is in elected legislatures. If the Constitution itself needs changing, it provides a way to make amendments, spelled out in Article V.

President Ronald Reagan summed it up this way:

> The role assigned to judges in our system was to interpret
> the Constitution and lesser laws, not to make them. It was to
> protect the integrity of the Constitution, not to add to it or
> subtract from it—certainly not to rewrite it. For as the framers
> knew, unless judges are bound by the text of the Constitution,
> we will, in fact, no longer have a government of laws, but of
> men and women who are judges. And if that happens, the
> words of the documents that we think govern us will be just
> masks for the personal and capricious rule of a small elite.[8]

IMMIGRATION

THE UNITED STATES' immigration system is broken in just about every way. "Broken" is really too mild a description. *Wrecked* is a better word. It's a system in ruins, and the federal government has been unwilling to do anything about it.

No one knows how many illegal immigrants are flooding across the southern border. Hundreds of thousands try each year. Most are from Mexico, but many come from El Salvador, Guatemala, Honduras, and other Latin American countries.

The Mexican border has become a lawless place. Illegal immigrants often pay "coyotes"—human smugglers—thousands of dollars to guide them across deserts and streams. Along the way, Mexican drug cartels often demand extortion money on threat of death. They kidnap thousands headed for the United States and hold them for ransom.

Many of the immigrants are children, sometimes traveling with parents, sometimes alone. Beatings, robberies, and rapes are part of the journey. People sometimes go days without food or water. Yet they risk it all because they've heard they can get into the United States.

When they reach the border, illegal immigrants try to slip past the Border Patrol. In some places they come in such huge numbers that overwhelmed agents can't stop them. Once on US soil, their chances of staying are good. If detained by authorities, they're often given a date to appear before an immigration judge and then released. Everyone knows they aren't likely to show up for the hearing.

Millions more who are here illegally come another way. They enter the country legally with a valid visa but then stay when their visa expires. They simply never go home.

It's impossible to tell exactly how many illegal immigrants are in this country. Some estimates put the number at twelve million and growing.[1] Since they broke the law entering the country, they live on the fringes of society. Most work in low-skill jobs, often using fake IDs and forged documents.

Meanwhile, millions around the world who want to come here legally can't because of official immigration limits. Because they want to play by the rules, they might wait years for permission to come to America, if permission ever comes at all.

It's a dysfunctional and dangerous state of affairs. And this is a country that likes to think of itself as immigrant friendly.

Why do conservatives want to keep immigrants out?

They don't. Most conservatives are strong supporters of *legal* immigration. They believe it's good for this country and the people coming here.

Immigration has always been an essential part of the American tradition. We are, after all, a nation built by immigrants and their children, grandchildren, and great-grandchildren. Immigrants make this a culturally rich land. They come with a strong work ethic and a determination to pursue the American Dream.

The United States has always played a special role in the world as a beacon of freedom. It's no accident that the Statue of Liberty, probably America's most famous monument, is a symbol of not only freedom but welcoming newcomers. Or that the words of the poet Emma Lazarus, inscribed on the statue's base, are some of our most beloved: "Give me your tired, your poor, your huddled masses yearning to breathe free, the wretched refuse of your teeming shore."

President Ronald Reagan summed up many conservatives' feelings this way: "I have always believed that this anointed land was set apart in an uncommon way, that a divine plan placed this great continent here between the oceans to be found by people from every corner of the Earth who had a special love of faith and freedom."[2]

On the other hand, conservatives take a strong stand against *illegal* immigration. There's a big difference between people going about something lawfully and going about it unlawfully.

People who want to immigrate here legally might stand in line for years to get a visa or green card. They fill out all the paperwork and often hire attorneys to help them navigate the system. That system is too complex and slow; it badly needs streamlining and reform. Nevertheless, this group goes about entering the country according to the rules.

Those who finally become citizens stand before a judge one day, raise their right hands, and take the oath of allegiance. For most, it's one of the proudest days of their lives.

At the same time, millions are sneaking in through the back door. They're looking for better lives, and that's understandable. But they start off by breaking the law and continue to break the law by staying illegally.

This isn't a matter of being anti-anybody or wanting to keep foreigners out. It's a matter of having sensible laws, enforcing them, and following them.

What's wrong with having an open border?

"What's wrong with open borders?" liberals sometimes say. "God has no borders. Neither should we. People should be free to go wherever they want."

A world without borders is a nice utopian dream, but it's not realistic. In fact, it would be dangerous.

Think about what would happen if you opened wide the door of your house or apartment and posted a sign that said, "Strangers Welcome—Come On In." Pretty soon you'd have people tromping in, making themselves at home, coming and going at will. You wouldn't feel safe, and for good reason. Eventually something bad would happen.

The same is true for a country. Leave the door wide open, and bad things will happen.

A porous border is a nightmare for law enforcement agencies. It means dealing with people who have false or no documentation. It risks letting in people who can make us unsafe. Tens of thousands of illegal immigrants in this country now are convicted criminals.[3]

People pouring over the border unchecked is a national security threat. We know that Islamic terrorists would like nothing better than to come into this country and kill as many Americans as they can. They've told us so, and there have been reports of Islamic terrorist cells operating along the southern border.

An open border increases the odds of diseases spreading from other places and quickly getting out of control. Masses of people surging in puts a strain on public finances. For example, children of illegal immigrants born here are automatically US citizens and are eligible for a wide range of welfare benefits.[4]

"Yes," someone might say, "but why worry about the southern border when we have miles of unprotected borders elsewhere? There are thousands of isolated places where someone could walk across the border from Canada or pull a boat into a coastal inlet." That's true, but the fact is that we don't have a problem of mass illegal immigration on those borders. We need to address the problem where it exists.

It's important to remember that Americans do, in fact, have the right to say, "This is our country. This is who we are and what we as a people believe. These are our sovereign borders, and we intend to maintain and defend them." Every country has the right to protect its borders as a way of protecting its identity. If it doesn't, it ceases to be its own country.

This nation especially has an interest in maintaining its sovereign borders. The United States is a special place. Millions want to come here for exactly that reason—because it's a special place. Americans want it to remain a beacon of freedom and opportunity for immigrants, and our rules should reflect that. But because so many want to come here, we need sensible limits, serious rules, and real borders.

Why don't we secure the border with Mexico?

We can if we choose to. It won't be easy or cheap, and we can't stop every single illegal entry, but the country certainly has the ability to have a much safer, more secure border.

"You'll never be able to get control over such a long border," some argue. They forget that after the terrorist attacks of September 11, 2001, the United States cut off virtually all illegal traffic for several weeks as a security measure. If we did it once, we can do it again.

Securing the border wouldn't mean a 2,000-mile-long fence. It would mean a combination of physical barriers, "virtual fences" made of cameras and sensors, and border patrols. Much of that system is already in place.

Securing the border would also mean a good "e-verify" system and strict enforcement to make sure employers aren't hiring illegal immigrants. Many illegal immigrants are here for work. If they know they can't get a job in the United States after jumping the border, they're much less likely to try.

Why hasn't the border been secured? Two groups have stood in the way: some business interests that want a steady flow of cheap labor, and politicians in both parties (but mainly Democrats) who want to curry the favor of the Hispanic community in hopes of building a permanent political majority.

Some immigration reformers support the idea of a guest worker program that allows foreign workers to enter the United States for a set period of time for jobs that need filling and then return to their home countries once their contracts have expired. A program like that may well be part of a long-term solution.

But securing the border is the first and essential step to any immigration reform. Until we have a border system that stops the lawlessness, requires people to enter the country in an orderly way, and keeps track of who is coming and going, we're going to keep having major problems.

Why not give amnesty to illegal immigrants who are already here?

"We let them in, so now we ought to let them stay." "Some of these people have spent decades building lives here. It would be heartless to make them leave now." "We're supposed to be a nation of immigrants. We can't deport twelve million people."

These are some arguments made in support of granting amnesty to people already here illegally. Feelings run high on this issue. People's futures are at stake, and it touches the question of what this country stands for.

Of course, many other Americans believe it's not right or smart to say, "Okay, you're here, so you can just stay." That amounts to rewarding people who have broken the law.

Granting amnesty also sends a message abroad: come in illegally, and eventually you'll get permission to stay. We learned that lesson after 1986, when Congress passed a law offering amnesty to millions. It ended up encouraging more illegal immigration.

Granting amnesty is a slap in the face to immigrants who have waited in line for years and have gone through the formal process to come here legally. It undermines the idea that laws actually mean something and that this nation's borders are sovereign.

Everyone recognizes that locating and deporting twelve million people would be extremely difficult, to say the least. It's not a prospect that anyone relishes.

Some reformers support the idea of a "path to citizenship" that would require people here illegally to pay fines and back taxes, learn English, and meet other conditions to earn the right to stay. Others argue that would give people who have broken the law one of the most sought-after privileges in the world—US citizenship.

The issue has huge political ramifications. Many Democratic lawmakers are, frankly, cynical in their calculations. They want to award citizenship to millions of illegal immigrants because they believe most would end up voting for Democrats.

As the debates continue, conservatives will look to uphold a handful of principles. We need to get control of our borders. We need a clear set of immigration laws, and people need to stick to them. That includes people who have come here illegally—they need to get right with the law. And for anyone who wants citizenship, priority should go to immigrants who have come here legally and patiently followed the rules.

Why do many conservatives want immigrants to learn English and "become American"?

Because if they don't, this country could end up falling apart.

Over the years, the United States has done a good job of assimilating immigrants—in other words, "Americanizing" them so they become part of our national family. That doesn't mean immigrants have to lose their heritage, whether it be Mexican, English, or Nigerian. It means coming to share ideals at the core of being American, principles like freedom of thought and speech, equality before the law, and the right to worship God as we please.

Those ideals make us all one people, no matter where we or our ancestors came from. They're the reason we have the Latin motto you see on every dollar bill and coin—*E pluribus unum*. Out of many, one.

Abraham Lincoln pointed out that American immigrants are heirs to the principles of the Declaration of Independence and other founding documents. The "moral sentiment" of 1776 is theirs to claim. "They have a right to claim it as though they were blood of the blood, and flesh of the flesh of the men who wrote that Declaration," Lincoln said.[5]

Is the country doing a good job of assimilating immigrants now? Maybe not as good as it used to. A 2011 survey found that only one in five Hispanics living here describe themselves as Americans.[6]

If immigrants don't come to think of themselves as Americans, this nation will eventually fracture or even dissolve. That's why conservatives believe it's crucial for schools to do a good job of teaching American history and civics. Yet test scores show that many schools *don't* do a good job of that.

Here's something else to think about. We live in a time when Islamic terrorists are recruiting people to do us harm. Their message is "Death to America." We don't want immigrants (or anyone else) living here to be open to such messages or to be the carriers of such messages.

We have to be realistic. If we want to be free of the hatred and violence that plague other parts of the world, America has to do a good job of assimilating its immigrants. We should want them to think of themselves as fellow citizens, to share our basic values.

It's also important for new Americans to learn English. Succeeding in this country without understanding English is difficult, and knowing it is a great asset for job advancement. The English language is part of the glue that holds us together. If we don't share a language, it's hard to share much else. That's just common sense.

This doesn't mean that English is better than any other language, or that Americans shouldn't speak second or third languages—that's a wonderful asset for anyone to have. But a basic requirement for any nation to stick together is that its citizens understand each other.

For generations, many people coming to these shores have made learning their new homeland's language one of their top goals. Their determination to speak English is part of the fabulous story of the American immigrant.

MARIJUANA

Dear Bill:

Please note when my son was 15 years old and sneaking marijuana I knew the destructive behavior and chaos that would ensue. My son is now 27 years old and a hopeless heroin addict living on the streets when he is not in prison. I have prayed and tried everything humanly possible at the cost of utter destruction of my family. Anyone that believes marijuana is harmless is like inviting your wife to have a boyfriend and believing things will be better in your marriage. Common sense is simple.

—GREG IN MICHIGAN, A LISTENER TO *Bill Bennett's Morning in America* NATIONAL TALK RADIO SHOW

YOU MAY KNOW SOMEONE LIKE GREG, a father who has had to watch drugs wreck his child's life. It's happening to millions as more and more young people smoke pot.

Something almost inexplicable is going on in our country right now. Two trend lines are moving in opposite directions in a way that defies common sense.

On the one hand, there's growing enthusiasm about making it legal for people to use marijuana. A handful of states have legalized it for recreational use, and several more for "medical use." A 2014 Gallup Poll found that about half of Americans favor legalizing marijuana.[1] That support cuts across political lines. It includes liberals as well as conservatives with strong libertarian streaks who believe they should have the personal freedom to use marijuana and that the government has no business telling them how to enjoy themselves.

Here's the stunning thing. While the push for legalization grows, scientific evidence about the dangers of marijuana piles up. The destruction in lives—people like Greg and his family—is piling up too.

This chapter explains some facts about marijuana usage and legalization, facts many people apparently don't know or are ignoring. It explores some questions about the limits of individual liberty when it comes to health and public safety. We summarize—and agree with—the arguments of conservatives who regard marijuana use as dangerous and wrong.

Take a look at the evidence; then do your own research. (And, no, we don't mean by lighting up.) For a more in-depth look at this subject, read the article "Adverse Health Effects of Marijuana Use" by Dr. Nora D. Volkow and others in the June 5, 2014, issue of the *New England Journal of Medicine*.

Don't just accept the arguments of those who want to legalize without some critical thinking and common sense. They're both much needed, because we live in a country where an awful lot of people have decided it's a good idea to legalize a dangerous drug.

Isn't pot harmless?

"It's not addictive like alcohol." "There are no bad side effects. It just makes you feel good, that's all." "My mom smoked it a lot when she was a kid, and it didn't hurt her."

You've probably heard statements like those or perhaps have made them yourself. Before you buy into them, there are some things you ought to know.

The first is that marijuana in the United States today is *several* times stronger than the marijuana people smoked in the 1970s and 1980s. Back then, marijuana was about 3 to 5 percent tetrahydrocannabinol (THC), the main psychoactive ingredient. The TCH levels of today's marijuana average around 13 percent but go as high as 20 percent and above.[2]

That means today's pot is a much more powerful drug. And it leads to many more health risks:

- **Marijuana literally alters the structure and function of the brain in young people.** The brain of a teenager is still growing. Introducing marijuana into it can actually change its normal development. Regular use affects receptors in the brain that are involved in a host of mental activities, from memory and appetite to pleasure response and pain tolerance. This is permanent, long-term damage to the brain.[3]
- **Regular use may make you permanently dumber.** We're not talking about just feeling mellow or goofy while high. We're talking about your ability to think for the rest of your life.

  Consider this opening line of a story from WebMD about scientific research on how marijuana affects IQ: "Cannabis users who start smoking the drug as adolescents show an irreparable decline in IQ, with more persistent use linked to a greater decline, new research shows." One of the researchers says, "Cessation of cannabis did not restore IQ among teen-onset cannabis users." In other words, once you lose that brain power, you don't ever get it back.[4]

- **Marijuana decreases motivation.** Long-term smokers tend to produce less dopamine, a chemical in the brain linked to motivation. Pot slowly robs people of their desire to learn, to grow, to push themselves. When that happens, school grades and job performance suffer.[5]
- **Marijuana smoke harms the lungs.** According to the American Lung Association, there are thirty-three cancer-causing chemicals in marijuana. Marijuana smoke also deposits tar into the lungs. The National Institute on Drug Abuse says that frequent marijuana smokers can develop many of the same problems as cigarette smokers, such as daily cough and phlegm production, more frequent acute chest illness, and a higher risk of lung infection.[6]
- **Marijuana increases the risks of heart problems.** Research links usage with the potential for cardiovascular disease, including heart attack, cardiac arrhythmia and stroke, and circulation problems in the arms and legs. "There is now compelling evidence on the growing risk of marijuana-associated adverse cardiovascular effects, especially in young people," the lead author of one study says.[7]
- **The short-term impact on judgment, coordination, and motor skills can be deadly.** More and more, marijuana is involved in fatal car crashes. Several researchers estimate that a driver has twice the risk of an automobile accident if there is any measurable amount of THC in the bloodstream.[8]
- **Marijuana use increases the risk of mental illness.** Those illnesses include psychosis, schizophrenia, anxiety, and

depression in adulthood.[9] "The link between cannabis and psychosis is quite clear now; it wasn't 10 years ago," says a prominent British neurobiologist.[10]

Marijuana users are fond of saying that one reason they like marijuana is that it's not addictive. That's false. While most people who try marijuana will not become addicted—just like most people who drink aren't addicted to alcohol—some users *do* become dope addicts.[11] According to the US Department of Health and Human Services, more than 4.4 million Americans age twelve and older meet the clinical criteria of marijuana dependence or abuse.[12] "There is no question that marijuana can be addictive; that argument is over," says a medical expert at the National Institute on Drug Abuse.[13]

There's also no question that for some users, marijuana is a "gateway drug" to even worse narcotics like cocaine and heroin. Not all marijuana users will go on to harder drugs, but almost all users of harder drugs started with marijuana. As the brain, especially the teen brain, gets used to the marijuana high, it needs more stimulation to get the same effect. That's when some users turn to the harder drugs. You can bet they started out thinking, *Marijuana's not going to hurt me.*[14]

Like it or not, millions of Americans enjoy smoking pot, so doesn't it make sense to just legalize it?

The big problem with legalizing marijuana is that more people would end up using it, not less. Is that really what we want?

Three factors have a big influence on drug use, especially youth drug use. The first is acceptability. The more society approves of a behavior, the more young people are apt to do it. Legalizing marijuana puts a stamp of acceptability on it, leading more people to try it.

The second factor is availability. The more available any product is, the easier it is to get hold of, the more people tend to use it. Making it legal to buy marijuana from a shop on Main Street definitely makes it more available.

The third factor is cost. As the supply of anything grows, the cost goes down. So as marijuana becomes more available with legalization, the cost drops, leading to more usage.[15]

It's not hard to imagine what kind of bad side effects a state is likely to get when pot is legal and easily available: more stoned drivers; more marijuana-related emergency room visits; more crime around places where marijuana is sold; more young people living on the streets. Officials in Colorado, where medical marijuana and recreational marijuana are both legal, say that's exactly what they're seeing.[16]

If nothing else, the widespread use of marijuana makes us a less capable people. California governor Jerry Brown voiced his objections to legalization this way: "How many people can get stoned and still have a great state or a great nation? The world's pretty dangerous, very competitive. I think we need to stay alert, if not twenty-four hours a day, more than some of the potheads might be able to put together."[17]

Alcohol and cigarettes are more harmful than marijuana and they're legal, so why shouldn't marijuana be?

This is a common argument: we've legalized two substances more harmful than marijuana—alcohol and cigarettes—so therefore we should legalize marijuana.

First of all, it's debatable whether alcohol and cigarettes are really more harmful than marijuana. Yes, drinking can destroy a life. So can cancer from cigarettes. But look again at the list of harms that marijuana can cause. It's a terrible list. This drug damages and destroys a lot of lives too.

Cigarettes can harm you over the long term, but marijuana, like alcohol, can harm you right away. People smoke it to get stoned. That loss of focus can mean worse performance at work or on school assignments. It can hurt or kill you while driving.

Even if alcohol and cigarettes *are* more harmful than marijuana, that still doesn't mean we should legalize marijuana. Making one more harmful substance legally available just adds to the problem.

It doesn't make any sense to say we should legalize an unhealthy product because something worse is already legal. That's like saying, "My house already has a hole in the roof, and that's worse than a broken window, so now I'm going to break a window."

Here's something to think about. One reason many teens use alcohol and tobacco is that those products are legal for adults, which makes them widely available. Teens see adults using them legally, which makes teens want to try them. There's every reason to think that if marijuana is legalized for adults and they use it more openly, it will drive teen usage up.

Here's something else to think about. Suppose cigarettes were not legal in the United States but were available only on the black market. Given all the health risks brought on by cigarettes—cancer, heart attack, stroke, emphysema, chronic bronchitis—would you vote to make them legal?

Of course, cigarettes *are* legal for adults to purchase. There's probably no putting that genie back in the bottle. But that doesn't mean we should let another one out.

Knowing all the problems we face with cigarettes and alcohol, does it make sense to make one more dangerous substance legal? It's simply not a good idea. We can add to the list of harmful products legally available in our country, or we can draw a line and say, "No more."

Shouldn't people have the right to decide what they do to their own bodies?

This is a question many libertarians ask. In their view, the government unfairly restricts people's freedom when it starts making laws about their eating or smoking habits.

"Even if marijuana is harmful," libertarians argue, "I'm not hurting anyone but myself. And whether or not I decide to harm myself is *my* business—not the government's. After all, it's my body."

But dangerous drugs cause much harm throughout society, and people who use them cause much harm to others. Once people use mind-altering drugs, they no longer think and act responsibly. That's one reason government makes laws about them.

Drug use brings high economic and social costs that affect everyone, not just the drug user. When people under the influence of marijuana commit crimes, it costs the victims. When they have car accidents, they injure or kill others. When they show up stoned for work or don't show up because they're stoned, it costs businesses in lost time and productivity. Drug-related emergency room visits and treatment programs drive up the costs of health care. Addictions to marijuana and other drugs bring terrible emotional costs to family members.

If the argument "It's my body, so it should be legal for me to put marijuana in it" is correct, then logic dictates that the same must be true for drugs like cocaine, heroin, and meth. Ask yourself, "Would the country be a better or worse place if we made those drugs legal to use, buy, and sell? And would legalizing drugs really make people freer?"

The argument for a right to marijuana really amounts to this: "I think I have the right to get stoned." At bottom, it's an argument based on self-gratification. There are much better causes to stand for. And much better ways to have fun.

Does marijuana help sick people?

Supporters of legalizing marijuana argue that it's useful for treating the pain associated with cancer, HIV, glaucoma, multiple sclerosis, and many other maladies. Some people claim it's good for whatever ails you, from anxiety to arthritis.

Several states have passed laws allowing the sale and use of "medical marijuana." In most of those states, a note from a doctor allows people to obtain a medical marijuana card. That card allows them to buy marijuana in shops known as "dispensaries" or "clinics."

What does the US scientific community have to say about the widespread use of marijuana as a medicine? Major medical associations take a very dim view of the idea, to say the least.

The American Medical Association, for example, says that "cannabis is a dangerous drug and as such is a public health concern."[18] The American Psychiatric Association says, "There is no current scientific evidence that marijuana is in any way beneficial for the treatment of any psychiatric disorder. In contrast, current evidence supports, at minimum, a strong association of cannabis use with the onset of psychiatric disorders."[19]

The idea that medical marijuana can be used for a long list of ailments is nowhere accepted in serious scientific literature.[20] So why in the world are medical marijuana shops doing booming business in places like Denver and Los Angeles?

In Denver, there are more medical marijuana dispensaries than Starbucks coffee shops, liquor stores, or licensed pharmacies. In Los Angeles, pot stores outnumber Starbucks and McDonald's combined by two to one.[21]

In states like Colorado and California, more than nine out of ten medical marijuana cardholders list "severe pain" as the reason they need marijuana. Most of those cardholders are men under age thirty-five.[22]

Do you really think all those young men are in "severe pain"? Here's a clue: some high schoolers joke that a medical marijuana card is a "get out of jail free card."[23]

Everyone knows what's really going on. The vast majority of purchases in marijuana medical dispensaries have nothing to do with medication. They're about people wanting to get high.

Some people with cancer, AIDS, or other serious diseases are in great pain and in need of relief. We all want them to have whatever help is available. Programs carefully monitored by doctors who prescribe marijuana for patients with those conditions may help ease real suffering.

But laws that make it easy for people to enjoy marijuana under the guise of "medical" needs aren't what they claim. They're just clever ways to legalize pot and make it widely available.

Is the war on drugs worth it?

The "war on drugs" is a decades-long campaign in America to reduce illegal drug use and trafficking. It's a campaign that involves many facets, from catching drug dealers to educating students about the dangers of drugs.

Many people who support legalizing marijuana say that the war on drugs is a failure. It has been a huge waste of time and money with few results, they argue. People are going to use drugs no matter what, so why bother?

Critics are right about one thing—in the last several years, the war on drugs has done little to reduce drug use, including marijuana. What those critics may not know is that America once made real progress in this fight.

In 1979, the United States reached a high-water mark of illegal drug use, with over 25 million users. (Over 23 million of them were marijuana users.) By 1992, we had reduced drug use to the low-water mark, 12 million users. We cut the number of drug users by more than half.[24]

How did that happen? Simply put, a lot of people focused hard on attacking the problem. Schools sent a strong anti-drug message to students. Government worked hard to stop drugs coming across the borders and put dealers in jail. There were lots of anti-drug TV commercials, and the news media gave intense coverage to the devastation caused by drugs. Movies helped signal that drug use was no longer "in."

The entire culture sent a strong message that drugs are wrong and mean trouble. But after a while that message relaxed and usage went back up. Today marijuana usage is creeping up to an all-time high. More teens smoke marijuana than tobacco cigarettes.[25]

With effort, we could reduce illegal drug use in America, just as we have before. Instead, during the last several years, the country has been going the opposite direction. We've seen a major cultural shift in attitudes toward drugs, especially marijuana. Much less attention is paid to the problem today. Marijuana is viewed by many as harmless and even medically beneficial.

In the view of many conservatives, abandoning the war on drugs is a tragic mistake. It means surrendering millions of people, especially young people, to less productive, impaired, and possibly disastrous lives.

Is using illegal drugs immoral?

This may be the most important question to ask about drugs. Unfortunately, it's a question that doesn't get talked about enough these days.

Using illegal drugs is obviously wrong in that it's breaking the law. But the question of right and wrong goes much deeper than that.

The late political scientist James Q. Wilson summed it up this way: "Drug use is wrong because it is immoral and it is immoral because it enslaves the mind and destroys the soul."[26] Drug use is wrong because of what it does to human character. It destroys people's moral sense, and it makes them less than they should be by burning away their sense of responsibility. The whole point of taking illegal drugs, after all, is to suspend reality, at least for a while. That includes suspending moral obligations.

People addicted to drugs neglect their duties. The lure can become so strong that they will do nothing else but take drugs. They will neglect everything in life that is important, noble, and worthwhile for the sake of drugs. Drugs make people bad family members and friends. They can make people disappoint and crush those who care about them. People addicted to drugs make bad employees and colleagues because drugs hurt their ability to give their best effort and be dependable.

Drugs make people bad citizens by destroying the civic virtues that a free society depends on, virtues like self-reliance, honesty, and individual responsibility. No self-governing society can function when its citizens are in a drug-induced haze. Buying illegal drugs also aids drug cartels, evil people, and enemies of our country.

Using drugs neglects and disappoints God. It's no way to treat our bodies, which are his creation.

When people forget that this is a moral issue, when they neglect to see right and wrong, they let down their guard, and that's when they get into trouble with drugs. Then they pay dearly.

RACE, CLASS, GENDER, *and* ETHNICITY

"CONSERVATIVES ARE greedy, hateful, bigoted people who want to take the country backward."

That's the cynical drumbeat the left has kept up for decades now.

To blacks, liberals have put out the message that conservatives (and Republicans in general) are cold-blooded people who don't care about minorities' rights and liberties. Vice President Joe Biden told African Americans that Republicans are "going to put y'all back in chains" with their economic policies.[1] Representative Charlie Rangel of New York has said of Republicans, "Some of them believe that slavery isn't over, and that they won the Civil War."[2]

To Hispanics, liberals have sent the message that being Hispanic and being Republican don't go together. "I don't know how anyone of Hispanic heritage could be a Republican, okay," Senator Harry Reid of Nevada told an audience of mostly Hispanic voters. "Do I need to say more?"[3]

To women, the left has said that conservatives are waging a "war on women," trying to take away their rights and put them back in the kitchen.

To middle- and low-income Americans, liberals have said that conservatives just want to slash taxes for the richest Americans and cut programs for the poor.

This is politics of the worst sort. It's the kind that divides people by race, ethnicity, gender, and class. It deliberately tries to set Americans against each other. Conservatives (or Republicans) are the villains, and blacks, Hispanics, women, gays, or any other minorities are the victims. It's the message given to many young people in classrooms around the country, especially in college courses that look at the world through the lens of race, gender, and class. It's also the message in left-slanted news stories, television shows, and movies.

Why? Largely for political gain—to build support for liberal policies and big government programs that will supposedly take care of all these victims and protect them from evil conservatives. The charges have been made for so long that many people believe them. It's a fear-mongering drumbeat. It's not good for the country, and it's just plain wrong.

Is the United States a racist, oppressive place?

"America is still a deeply racist country." "Legal racism is gone, but it doesn't matter because racism is entrenched in every part of American life." "People who oppose President Obama just can't stand the color of his skin."

Sometimes you'll hear and read these kinds of statements coming from the left. Conservatives don't buy them. They know their country is a lot better than that.

Yes, bigotry and racism still exist among Americans of all colors. Sometimes shameful incidents of racism break into the news, and they're always widely denounced. They're denounced because racist views aren't representative of the country as a whole—of conservatives, liberals, Democrats, or Republicans.

Yes, this country has some chapters in its past that include the terrible treatment of some groups. Racism was once widespread throughout white America. Its effects devastated millions of lives.

But America today is not the America of fifty, one hundred, or two hundred years ago. No other country has done more to secure the rights and liberties of minorities. In today's America, people generally treat each other with respect and fairness—much more so than in many other parts of the world. The vast majority of Americans want nothing but the best for their fellow Americans.

That includes conservative Americans. When Democratic researchers studied white conservative Republican voters in Georgia soon after Barack Obama's election, they found that the conservatives' opposition to President Obama had everything to do with his policies and nothing to do with his race. The color of his skin simply was not important, "indeed, was almost beside the point," they concluded.[4]

Some young people today have a hard time fathoming the kind of racism they read about in history books. They ask their parents and grandparents, "Did people really hate other people because of their race? Did they really treat each other that way?" That's how far we've come.

Is there more work to be done? Absolutely. But we should be proud of the progress made in the last several decades.

Condoleezza Rice, an African American woman from Alabama who served as US Secretary of State, among other high offices, summed it up well:

> The fact of the matter is we're not race-blind. Of course we
> still have racial tensions in the country. But the United States

of America has made enormous progress in race relations, and it is the best place on earth to be a minority. . . . To my mind, the great thing about the United States of America is that you can be of any color, any ethnic group, any nationality, any religion and you can have dreams and aspirations that are your own, and then you can pursue them. That's what this country's about.[5]

Barack Obama reaffirmed that point when he was elected the nation's first African American president in 2008. On the night of his election, he said, "If there is anyone out there who still doubts that America is a place where all things are possible; who still wonders if the dream of our founders is alive in our time; who still questions the power of our democracy, tonight is your answer."[6]

Are conservatives against diversity?

Of course not, despite what liberals sometimes say or imply. One of the things that makes this such a great country is that it's full of people with ancestries and backgrounds from all over the world. We draw strength from our diversity. As the poet Walt Whitman wrote, "Here is not merely a nation but a teeming nation of nations."[7]

Diversity makes this country a much more interesting place to live. There are few parts of the world outside the United States where you can find restaurants serving Chinese, Italian, Mexican, French, Indian, Thai, and Lebanese food all in one small town. Or hear Irish ballads in a pub one night and jazz rooted in African American music the next. It's all commonplace here.

Your heritage is part of who you are. History and traditions matter—that's one of the beliefs central to conservatism. The best traditions of your family and community need to be preserved.

The problem comes when we focus on our differences so much

that we let them divide us. We begin to think of one another mainly in terms of ethnicity or class—as one of *them* instead of one of *us*.

As important as race and ethnicity are, they are not the essence of who each of us is. As the Reverend Martin Luther King Jr. used to say, it's not the color of our skin but the content of our character that matters.

The real danger comes when people use race, ethnicity, and other differences to turn groups against each other for political gain. That's politics of division, the kind that sends the message, "That group over there wants to do your group harm." Black vs. white. Men vs. women. The rich vs. the rest. Diversity becomes not a reason for celebration but a cause of resentment. The politics of division make people think of themselves as victims who have been oppressed by others. It leads them to think the worst of people who are different.

E pluribus unum, one of the mottos on every US coin, is an excellent guide. "Out of many, one." Our diversity comes from the *pluribus*—the many skin colors, backgrounds, and traditions we bring together. That's all to be celebrated.

The *unum* is the crowning part, though, the most important part. In the end, we should think of ourselves as one people.

Is affirmative action for blacks and other minorities a good idea?

Affirmative action is a policy that dates back to the 1960s in the United States. In its original form, it meant that employers should cast a wide net and seek out qualified minority candidates when hiring. The aim was to end discrimination in hiring and make sure minorities got the same chance at jobs as everyone else.

Over time, affirmative action changed into something quite different. It became a policy that requires employers to give a certain percentage of jobs to minorities. It also refers to college admission policies that take race into account when accepting students so that minorities make up a certain percentage of a student body. Affirmative action is sometimes called set-asides, quotas, or preferential treatment.

The theory behind preferential treatment is that because of historical discrimination, blacks and other minorities are at a disadvantage when it comes to applying for jobs or getting into college. To erase that disadvantage, standards may be lowered for them. For example, a college might accept black students with lower grades and SAT scores than white or Asian students.

The intentions behind this are good, but most conservatives believe that kind of affirmative action is wrong. It tries to remedy past discrimination by setting up a new system of discrimination, one that favors certain groups over others because of skin color, gender, or ethnic background. You don't get rid of discrimination by making discrimination an official policy.

The unspoken assumption behind preferential treatment is that minorities can't compete without lower standards. That may have been true several decades ago, when they were denied basic rights and decent educations, but it's a terrible assumption to make today. There have been countless examples of minorities achieving success in every field.

Preferential treatment by race isn't only demeaning, it's unfair. It brands minorities as less than capable. It causes resentment when some students (who have never discriminated against anyone else) realize it will be harder for them to get into college than somebody else with a favored skin color.

It can also be unfair to minorities who get into tough colleges even though they have lower scores and grades. Once they're in, they may find out they're really not prepared. That's setting people up for failure. Too often they end up dropping out.

This country won't work without diversity in its workplaces and on its college campuses. Affirmative action in its original form is a good idea. Employers need to reach out to minority communities, recruit aggressively in them, and encourage their members to apply for jobs.

Colleges need to get scholarship money and loans to qualified students from poor families. Most important, all Americans need access to good schools at the K–12 level so they can be well qualified for college and careers.

But any system that gives or takes points from people because of their race, gender, or ethnicity is wrong. The way to achieve a color-blind society is to *be* a color-blind society, in law and spirit.

Is the upper class evil?

Greedy. Unethical. Uncaring. Destructive.

That pretty much sums up the way the left often portrays wealthy people, especially wealthy businesspeople. They take most of the money and leave "everybody else scrambling for the crumbs," as one liberal filmmaker put it.[8]

Before we start throwing bricks at fellow Americans, here are a few thoughts to keep in mind.

First, most affluent people in America got that way through hard work.[9] Their wealth is the product of a system where people are free to succeed. The alternative is government controlling how much people make, with less freedom to succeed.

Demonizing any segment of the population is wrong, and that includes demonizing people who have more money than you or I. It's class warfare, and it's ugly because it plays on envy.

Here's something to think about. The "upper class" isn't a fixed group of people in the United States. Americans move up and down the income scale all the time. Nearly three out of four American adults will spend at least one year in the top 20 percent of income earners.[10]

In other words, many high-income earners haven't always earned so much money and may not always do so. They're ordinary Americans like the rest of us, not a special breed that deserves scorn.

One problem today is that many people feel like upward mobility is breaking down. For many in the middle and lower classes, wages haven't been rising like they have in the past. People feel like they are treading water financially, if not starting to drown. That's what happens when the economy is weak or the education system doesn't do a good job.

Another problem is a widening "wealth gap" between how much the very rich and everyone else makes. That can cause frustration and bitterness among people struggling to get ahead.

But the answer isn't to tear down people who have done well. The answer is to make sure everyone has the opportunity to rise. Chances are good that with hard work and a bit of luck, you'll find yourself doing well financially someday. That's one of the promises of America. If we demonize success, we'll wear down the spirit that has made this country the land of opportunity.

How do conservative values help women and minorities?

They help the same way they help anyone else—"conservative" values apply to all. Conservatives don't look at the world in terms of "those values are right for this group, other values are better for that group."

The traditional moral values conservatives care deeply about—virtues like personal responsibility, hard work, integrity, faith—are values that make a good life for anyone. The more people put stock in them, the better the country is.

Conservatives champion institutions that cross ethnic, gender, and political lines, institutions that benefit all people. Free enterprise, for example, has done more to create jobs and lift people into prosperity than any economic system in history. A strong free enterprise system coupled with equal opportunities for all means more success for minorities.

One reason conservatives are so concerned about the state of the American family is that success in life is linked to strong, intact families. It doesn't matter what color or class those families are.

One reason conservatives have pushed for higher expectations for *all* students is that they know a good education is the best equalizer. It's why they want minority families in neighborhoods with bad schools to have more choice about where they send their children to school.

You can go through life buying into an ideology that views this country as a place where one group is always trying to victimize another. Or you can view it as a place where we celebrate our diversity and draw strength from it.

You can see life through a prism that divides people into classes always struggling with each other. Or you can focus on qualities in people that transcend race and class.

You can think of the country as a place devoted to group rights based on race, sex, or income. Or you can see it as a place devoted to the idea of protecting the individual rights of every American.

It has been said that there are really only two races of people, decent and indecent.[11] That's a much better way to look at the world than obsessing over the color of people's skin or how much money they're making.

Part 4

NATIONAL DEFENSE

NATIONAL
DEFENSE

THE ANCIENT GREEK COLONY OF Sybaris was once a flourishing place. Set on Italy's southern coast, it possessed a fine port and rich surrounding countryside. The Sybarites carried on a prosperous trade with cities around the Mediterranean, and over time they built an immense fortune. The wealthier they became, however, the more time they spent feasting and dreaming up new ways to entertain themselves.

One day a flute player came up with the idea of teaching horses to dance. The Sybarites had one of the finest cavalries in that part of the world, and before long the sound of a pipe set every warhorse in the army prancing away. The entire city would turn out to enjoy the spectacle and dance along with the horses.

Nearby lay the town of Croton. For quite a while its people had looked with envy on the rich lands and treasures of Sybaris and several times had waged war on the Sybarites, but the small Croton army was no match for the Sybarite cavalry. Then a spy reported to the Crotoniates that he had seen the Sybarite horses dancing to a flute.

The Crotoniates knew just what to do. They sent their army to attack the Sybarites. At the front marched a company of farmers and shepherds armed with nothing but flutes. The Sybarite cavalry galloped out to meet them, expecting an easy victory, but as soon as the Crotoniate pipes struck up a tune, the Sybarite warhorses began to caper. They waltzed to the music while the Crotoniate army swept the field, and Sybaris fell.

The story, recorded by the ancient writer Athenaeus in the third century, may at first seem like just a quaint old legend, but Athenaeus wrote it down because it contains ageless wisdom. Even in the twenty-first century—*especially* in the twenty-first century—a nation that is in many ways the envy of the world has much to lose if it lets its defenses down.

Why does America need such a big, powerful military?

The world is full of threats to American security. Islamic terrorist groups like al-Qaeda and ISIS (the Islamic State of Iraq and Syria) continue their jihad against the West. Iran, the chief sponsor of terror in the Middle East, is on the verge of becoming a nuclear power. Its government routinely sends crowds into the streets to chant "Death to America!" North Korea is a nuclear power. Its totalitarian dictatorship is ruthless, secretive, and unpredictable. Boko Haram, based in Nigeria, wages terror against all.

China's communist government is building up its military and could threaten US allies in Asia. Russian troops rolling into the Crimean Peninsula in 2014 have raised the specter of Cold War–era Soviet aggression in Europe.

Americans have much to lose from such threats in the way of

material possessions. But we have something even more precious and vulnerable that needs protecting: freedom. It's a mistake to take it for granted. As the great nineteenth-century statesman Daniel Webster put it, "God grants liberty only to those who love it, and are always ready to guard and defend it."[1]

The founders understood this notion well. That's why, in the preamble of the Constitution, they stated that one of the main reasons for establishing a new government was to "provide for the common defense."

Defense is arguably the first and chief responsibility of the federal government. No other institution is capable of protecting the country from foreign attack. John Jay, one of the nation's most important founders, put it this way: "Among the many objects to which a wise and free people find it necessary to direct their attention, that of providing for their *safety* seems to be the first."[2]

The best way to preserve both our safety and our freedom is to maintain a powerful military to answer threats wherever they may arise—a policy known as "peace through strength." The policy does not mean having a large army in order to conquer territory or start wars. It means that maintaining a powerful military discourages enemies from attacking us because we possess the might to overwhelm them.

The concept of peace through strength has been around for a long time, no doubt since the days of Sybaris. George Washington, in his first State of the Union message to Congress, said that "to be prepared for war is one of the most effectual means of preserving peace."[3] In 1980, when Ronald Reagan accepted the Republican presidential nomination, he reminded us that a strong United States military helps the cause not only of peace but of freedom:

> We are not a warlike people. Quite the opposite. We always
> seek to live in peace. We resort to force infrequently and

with great reluctance—and only after we have determined that it is absolutely necessary. We are awed—and rightly so—by the forces of destruction at loose in the world in this nuclear era. But neither can we be naive or foolish. Four times in my lifetime America has gone to war, bleeding the lives of its young men into the sands of beachheads, the fields of Europe and the jungles and rice paddies of Asia. We know only too well that war comes not when the forces of freedom are strong, but when they are weak. It is then that tyrants are tempted.[4]

Reagan used the doctrine of peace through strength to lead the free world during the Cold War. He knew that the Soviet Union could not stand up to the pressure of a US military buildup and a hard stance against totalitarianism. The Soviet empire collapsed, and tens of millions of people were liberated from the tyranny of communism.

Has the US military done more good or harm over time?

"US foreign policy is soaked in blood." "The American war machine is a death machine." "The flag stands for jingoism and vengeance and war."

These sorts of statements come from far-left critics of the United States, critics abroad and critics here at home. It's not uncommon to run across them on college campuses or in high-school classrooms. These critics speak from a deep conviction that American power has done much harm overseas. They often insist that the United States is an "imperialist" or "colonialist" power, wreaking its evil will on the people of the third world. Their condemnation represents a profound misreading of history.

On balance, the US military is an enormous force for good in the world. During the Revolutionary War, Americans fought to establish the first nation created so people could be free. During the Civil War, the Union Army fought to preserve government by the people and to end American slavery. During World War I, Americans fought in the trenches of Europe to help stop a catastrophe that was engulfing much of the world.

During World War II and then the Cold War, the United States led the way in saving the world from catastrophe. A group of European prime ministers and presidents put it this way in a letter published in 2003 in the *Wall Street Journal*: "Thanks in large part to American bravery, generosity and farsightedness, Europe was set free from the two forms of tyranny that devastated our continent in the 20th century: Nazism and communism."[5]

In this century, American soldiers have bled in Afghanistan and Iraq to combat terrorism and end brutal regimes that subjugated millions. Over the decades, the US military has launched countless humanitarian and relief efforts, from aiding victims of natural disasters to rescuing ships at sea.

America's record is not spotless. There have been times when the US military was used for injustice, such as the forced removal of Native Americans from ancestral lands. And tragedy has come with every war. For example, there have been US drone attacks against terrorists in Afghanistan that, despite the military's best efforts, have killed innocent civilians.

But it's important to remember that throughout history other superpowers have used armies to conquer territory and build empires by force. America, with its unrivaled military, has chosen a different course. The fact is that the United States has liberated more people from tyranny than any other nation in history.

If you live in some desperate part of the world with a dictator's boot on your neck and you see a group of men coming over the hill with a flag, you hope and pray it's the American flag. Because the

American soldier is a soldier you can be absolutely confident is there to help you.

The United States is the greatest defender of freedom in the world. It's a record every American can be proud of.

Can we afford to spend so much money on the military?

This is a question thoughtful people on both the right and the left are asking. America's staggering debt means that every part of the federal budget, including defense, has to be scrutinized. But if defense spending is cut too deeply, it will endanger our safety.

The wars in Iraq and Afghanistan have been enormously expensive. Military operations have cost taxpayers more than one and a half trillion dollars.[6] But it's not true, as some on the left like to claim, that defense spending is the main cause of federal debt. As the chart below shows, over the last several decades defense spending has declined as a percentage of the Gross Domestic Product, while spending on

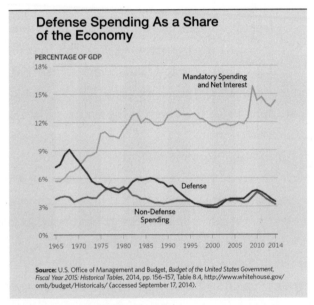

Graph courtesy of The Heritage Foundation

entitlements like Social Security, Medicare, and Medicaid, as well as interest payments on the national debt, has gone up.[7]

In 2014, to save money, the Obama administration proposed cutting the army to its smallest size since before World War II. President Obama's secretary of defense stated that "we are entering an era where American dominance on the seas, in the skies and in space can no longer be taken for granted."[8] That's an unnerving thought for many around the globe.

Here's another sobering thought. China and Russia are both building their militaries as we cut ours. The United States still spends more on defense, but China and Russia clearly aim to close the gap.

Not only are China and Russia building their militaries, but they've begun to cooperate with a "high-level of mutual trust," according to the Chinese defense ministry.[9] A Chinese-Russian military alliance is very bad news for freedom. Their combined strength could pose a serious threat. We need to be ready for it.

Generally speaking, liberals are less interested than conservatives in spending money on the military. They'd rather devote funds to social programs such as education or welfare. Conservatives answer that if we don't adequately defend ourselves, everything else the government does may be for naught.

Yet conservatives, especially fiscal conservatives, recognize that we face hard choices about military spending. This topic will be much debated in coming years. As the debate proceeds, conservatives will remind people that in the ranking of the federal government's responsibilities, protecting our nation is at the top.

Shouldn't the United States simply defend its own shores and keep its troops closer to home?

"Other nations would like us better if we'd scale back our army and stop trying to lead the world." "The world would be better off without a military superpower." "The United States should stop try-ing to be the world's policeman."

After so many years of fighting in Iraq and Afghanistan, some people think the era of America as "leader of the free world" needs to end. It's time for our military to stay closer to home, they say.

One answer to these arguments is that it's better to fight enemies overseas when necessary than to have them attack us here at home. We learned that painful lesson on September 11, 2001.

Another answer is that sooner or later, some other nation—China, for example—will become a military superpower. Would the world be better off if China, a nation that has little respect for human rights, had the most powerful military?

A third answer is that when freedom doesn't have a champion, aggressors move into the vacuum. For example, when the United States completely withdrew its forces from Iraq in 2011 after fight-ing so hard there, the brutal terrorist organization ISIS seized large parts of the country.

There will always be ruthless people and governments that try to take what they can by force, including other people's liberty. The United States, more than any other nation, has tied itself to the idea of standing up for liberty.

The United States can't rush to every trouble spot. We should always be reluctant to send Americans into combat. Such action should come as a last resort.

But when forces of evil take hold, they'll keep growing unless a strong force for good stops them. If a serious threat to freedom rises, the United States is the sole global power that can stand up to it. The world is a freer, safer place with a strong America.

Sergeant Alvin York, the reluctant hero who left his Tennessee plow during World War I to fight overseas, was asked the question "What did war get you?" when he got home. He answered this way: "The thing they forget is that liberty and freedom and democracy are so very precious that you do not fight to win them once and stop. . . . Liberty and freedom and democracy are prizes awarded only to those peoples who fight to win them and then keep fighting eternally to hold them."[10]

ISLAMIC
TERRORISM

Islamic terrorist groups now operate throughout much of the world. If you want to know what they intend for us, take a look at the group known as the Islamic State of Iraq and Syria (ISIS).

In 2014 ISIS declared itself a caliphate—a Muslim state ruled by the successor of the prophet Muhammad—after overrunning large parts of Syria and Iraq. Its leader, who calls himself the caliph, told followers that they will "conquer Rome and own the world, if Allah wills."[1]

ISIS counts tens of thousands of well-armed fighters in its army, including some Americans and Europeans who have traveled to the Middle East to join its ranks. They have slaughtered anyone who gets in their way.

ISIS militants have seized towns and forced thousands of men, women, and children to flee for their lives. They have murdered whole families, kidnapped and raped women, and sold women as sex slaves. They have buried children and young people alive.

Public executions are commonplace. They line people up by the score, taunt them, then shoot them in the head. Sometimes they shove the bodies into mass graves, sometimes they leave them lying in the sun. Some bodies have been tied to makeshift crosses and left as warnings.

"It is like a waterfall of blood," one eyewitness to killings said. "There are more and more executions and now the children watch like they are used to it."[2]

Religious leaders say that the persecution of Christians in ISIS-controlled regions has become a genocide. Churches have been burned, crosses and statues of the Virgin Mary attacked, ancient books and artifacts destroyed. The destruction has included sites holy to Jews as well as Muslims who do not adhere to ISIS theology. In July 2014 ISIS members blew up the tomb of the prophet Jonah in Iraq's northern city of Mosul.

ISIS members have burned captives alive. They have cut off the heads of innocent Westerners, including Americans, and proudly posted the videos on the Internet. They run terrorism schools where boys as young as eight practice beheading people. "It was like learning to chop an onion," one teenager reported. "You grab him by the forehead and then slowly slice across the neck."[3]

"Today our swords are unsheathed towards you, government and citizens alike!" ISIS has warned Americans. "And we will not stop until we quench our thirst for your blood."[4]

Who are the terrorists targeting the United States?

Most terrorism against the United States has been committed by Islamic radicals who want to force their interpretation of Muslim teaching and law on others. These terrorists hate everything the

United States stands for. We know this because they proudly tell us so every time they kill.

Islamic terrorist groups operate in the Middle East and Africa, in Europe, in Central and Southeast Asia, and beyond. They have become adept at recruiting followers through the Internet. In addition to ISIS, the most notorious groups include al-Qaeda ("the base"); Hamas ("zeal") in the Gaza Strip; Hezbollah ("Party of Allah") in Lebanon and Syria; Boko Haram (loosely translated, "Western education is a sin") in Nigeria and nearby regions; and the Taliban ("students") in Afghanistan and northwest Pakistan.

These groups make up a fraction of the 1.6 billion Muslims worldwide. The majority of Muslims have nothing to do with terrorism, nor do they want to have anything to do with it. But even a fraction of 1.6 billion means untold numbers bent on jihad. They can murder a lot of people. (On September 11, 2001, we learned what just nineteen terrorists can do.) Furthermore, a significant minority of Muslims overseas—millions of people in some nations—sympathize at least in part with Islamic terrorists' acts and worldview.[5]

The word *jihad* means "struggle" in Arabic, and in Islam the term is sometimes used to describe an inner struggle to live a moral life. To most people, however, and certainly to Islamic radicals, the term means something quite different—"holy war." Jihad is exactly what Osama bin Laden, mastermind of the attacks against the World Trade Center and Pentagon on September 11, 2001, had in mind when he called on "every Muslim who believes in God and hopes for reward to obey God's command to kill the Americans and plunder their possessions."[6]

The aim of jihadists is to wreak havoc on Western nations, especially the United States, or "the Great Satan," as they call us. In Arab regions, they are bent on annihilating the state of Israel. Wherever they gain power, Islamic radicals oppress not only Westerners and non-Muslims but also "deviant" Muslim leaders who do not follow the radicals' beliefs. They are determined to impose totalitarian rule on Muslim lands and extend Islamic dominion over the world.

Why do Islamic terrorists attack us?

There has been much theorizing about the root causes of Islamic terrorism. Some suggest it springs up in cultures overwhelmed by poverty, ignorance, and despair and that the best way to end terrorism is to raise people's hopes and prospects, because striking back only embitters them more.

Raising hopes and prospects is a worthy goal, but the problem with that theory is that many terrorists come from middle-class backgrounds or better. Wealthy, privileged people like Osama bin Laden often mastermind or finance terrorist operations.

Islamic terrorists claim that they act in response to the sins of the United States and other Western nations, such as publishing pornography and establishing military bases in Saudi Arabia. They assert that United States foreign policy is imperialistic, that its war machine is the greatest threat to world peace. They make these claims even as they enslave women and slaughter "infidels" who do not share their beliefs.

In fact, American soldiers have put themselves in harm's way to defend or liberate millions of Muslims in Iraq, Kuwait, Saudi Arabia, Bosnia, Kosovo, Somalia, Afghanistan, and other countries. They have fought to save more Muslims from tyranny than any other military in modern history. It is the terrorists who threaten to destroy the West and replace it with an Islamic empire, not the other way around.

Some say that America's support of Israel is a main cause of terrorists' rage against us. True, Islamic radicals have nothing but hatred for Israel (the "Little Satan," as they call it). But there is no reason to think that if the United States abandoned Israel, a staunch democratic ally, terrorists would suddenly grow fond of the "Great Satan" and stop their war against the "decadent" West.

Islamic terrorists are driven by a manic determination to force their religion and law on others. This is, at bottom, the age-old struggle between tyranny and freedom. Islamic radicals hate the freedom represented by Western democracy and will do all they can to replace it with their rule.

Faisal Shahzad, a Pakistani-American who tried and failed to explode a bomb in Times Square in 2010, told us exactly what his aim was. He told a judge, "If I am given a thousand lives, I will sacrifice them all for the sake of Allah fighting this cause, defending our lands, making the word of Allah supreme over any religion or system. . . . The defeat of U.S. is imminent and will happen in the near future, inshallah ["Allah willing"], which will only give rise to much awaited Muslim caliphate, which is the only true world order."[7]

What is life under the rule of Islamic radicals like?

The reports coming out of territories controlled by ISIS offer a glimpse. Iran, a nation that exports terrorism to the world, offers another.

In Iran, speech is restricted and, when opposed to the state, curtailed and violently punished. Radio and TV broadcasts are state controlled. Books are vetted by the "Ministry of Culture." Freedom of assembly is prohibited. Islamic law—sharia—permits flogging, amputation, and execution by stoning or hanging for various social and political offenses.[8]

In the 1980s, during its war with Iraq, Iran's leadership sent thousands of preteens and teenagers to clear minefields by walking through them and blowing themselves to pieces. The children were given little plastic keys to carry with them to unlock paradise after the mines exploded.[9]

In 2014 Iran's supreme leader, Ayatollah Ali Khamenei, declared that jihad against America would go on. "This battle will only end when the society can get rid of the oppressors' front with America at the head of it, which has expanded its claws on human mind, body and thought," he told members of Iran's parliament.[10]

In the most repressive Islamic regimes, young people are punished for listening to Western music or wearing Western clothes, women are assaulted for not covering their bodies and faces in public, girls are prohibited from going to school, women who commit adultery are stoned to death, women are forced to undergo involuntary genital surgery, homosexuals are executed, ancient and priceless works of art are destroyed if deemed anti-Islamic, and children are taught that Jews are pigs and monkeys.

Violence and murder are glorified. As one radical Islamic cleric declared in a television sermon on Palestinian television, "Blessings to whoever put a belt of explosives on his body or on his sons' and plunged into the midst of the Jews."[11]

Islamic radicals spread their faith at gunpoint. In 2014, for example, the terrorist group Boko Haram kidnapped some 275 girls, many of them Christians, from a school in Chibok, Nigeria. The Christians were offered a choice: convert to Islam or die. Many of the girls were reportedly sold into slavery or forced into marriages. Boko Haram continues its rampage of massacres and kidnappings in northeast Nigeria and surrounding areas.

Should we use terms like "Islamic extremists" and "jihadists"?

The first necessary step in this fight is to call things what they really are, by their proper names. Some politicians and pundits—particularly liberal ones—are reluctant to use phrases like "jihadists" and "Islamic extremists." They prefer terms like "violent extremists" and "individuals who commit violence." They seem quick to describe terrorist attacks as "isolated" or "lone wolf" operations.

In other words, they don't want to imply that terrorism is connected to Islam. Their reluctance is often based on political correctness. They don't want to be seen as criticizing or judging another culture in any way. They say they don't want to use language that might give people the idea that this is a religious war. They fear that talk of "Islamic terrorism" might bring retribution against innocent Muslims.

The problem with their political correctness is that it's not in line with reality. Most terrorism in the world today is very much connected to radical Islam. It may be a warped version of Islam, but when terrorists are putting "infidels" to the sword because they don't follow sharia law and are shouting "*Allahu Akbar*" ("Allah is the greatest") as they blow themselves and others to pieces, it makes no sense to pretend that things are not what they are. The reality is this: the majority of Muslims in the world are peaceful, but over the last twenty years many horrific terrorist acts have been committed in the name of Islam.

It also makes no sense to hope against hope that each new attack is the work of one or two demented people acting in isolation, unconnected to a larger ideology. They certainly may be demented, and they may build bombs alone, but terrorists are usually connected in mind and spirit. In this age of the Internet, they are often very connected to Islamic terrorists in other lands.

Why is it important to call our enemies by what they are? It's important because if we don't, we risk our own destruction. If we don't recognize our enemies, then we open ourselves all the more to danger. If we ignore their real motives and intentions, we can't defend ourselves as well.

These are not enemies who will lay down their swords because we speak delicately. They view mealymouthed talk as a sign of weakness, and that makes them want to attack us all the more.

What is the best way for the United States to respond to Islamic terrorism?

Jihadists are at war with us, and they have vowed to keep it up. They post threats on Facebook and Twitter such as "we are in your state / we are in your cities / we are in your streets. You are our goals anywhere."[12] ISIS has promised that "we will raise the flag of Allah in the White House."[13]

The United States must fight back as hard as it can. There really is no other choice when facing a dangerous enemy that is determined to destroy us.

This is a time when moral clarity is much needed—a time when Americans need to distinguish clearly between right and wrong. Radical Islam is evil staring us in the face, threatening to wipe out all we hold to be good. When good people fail to recognize evil for what it is, when they fail to meet it head-on with strength, evil has a way of overcoming good.

This is an enemy that thrives on weakness and appeasement. "Dealing with the pampered and effeminate Americans will be easy," Osama bin Laden predicted before the attacks on September 11, 2001.[14] He was wrong about America's response to 9/11. Unfortunately, however, the United States has sometimes failed to respond forcefully to terrorism.

A classic example is the September 11, 2012, attack on the woefully unprotected American consulate in Benghazi, Libya, which killed US ambassador Christopher Stevens and three other Americans. The Obama administration initially claimed the attack was not terrorism but rather an uprising caused by an anti-Muslim video circulating on the Internet. That story proved to be false. The United States then vowed to punish those responsible for the attack but moved very slowly in efforts to hunt down the attackers.[15]

That kind of response only encourages terrorists. Tyrants prey on uncertainty and weakness. They generally do not attack where and when they think they will lose.

This is a long struggle. The only way this nation will have the perseverance to continue the fight is if we remember what we are fighting for.

The United States has provided more freedom to more people than any nation in history; it has provided a greater degree of equality to more people than any nation in history; it has created more prosperity and spread it more widely than any nation in history; it has brought more justice to more people than any in history. Our open, tolerant, prosperous, peaceable society is the marvel and envy of the ages.

Consider this: there is no Muslim country where Muslims can enjoy more political, religious, or economic freedom than they can in the United States. That is to our credit, and probably to our enemies' resentment as well.

We cannot take our rights and freedom for granted, because Islamic radicals have sworn to bring jihad against them. If we do not defend ourselves strenuously and fight back against those who intend to destroy us, we ourselves will be destroyed.

Part 5

TRADITIONAL VALUES

TRADITIONAL VALUES

ONE OF THE MOST STRIKING IMAGES in classical literature is from the Roman poet Virgil, who lived in the first century BC. His epic *The Aeneid* tells the story of how the Trojan hero Aeneas leaves Troy after its fall to the Greeks, wanders for years with a band of survivors, and finally establishes a new home in Italy, where his descendants found Rome.

The image comes on the night of Troy's destruction, after the crafty Greeks have slipped out of the belly of their great wooden horse and taken the city by surprise. Aeneas tries to drive them back but soon realizes it's hopeless, so he rushes home to save his family.

He tells his aged father, Anchises, to gather their Penates, little statues of their household gods that represent their most cherished customs and beliefs. He then hoists his father onto his shoulders, takes his boy Ascanius by the hand, and makes his way through the flaming city into the countryside.

Artists have depicted the scene for centuries: one generation carrying the older generation, along with the traditions and values that will be handed down to the younger generation when they eventually reach their new home.

This passing of wisdom and traditional values from one generation to the next lies at the heart of conservatism. The word *conservative* comes from the Latin word *conservare*, meaning to keep safe, observe, or maintain. Every generation has the responsibility of preserving our best values, along with the customs and institutions that help pass those values to the next generation.

When one generation fails to pass along traditional values, things can go very wrong. It leaves people without a clear sense of what's important, of the difference between right and wrong. That can ruin lives and harm entire cultures.

What are "traditional values"?

First and most important, traditional values include good moral values—old-fashioned virtues like honesty, courage, compassion, and responsibility. The moral values you hold make all the difference in how good your life is. That truth of the human condition has never changed and will never change.

Conservatives believe there are enduring moral truths in the universe. That is, there are rules of right and wrong behavior that have come down to us through the centuries and apply to all. Moral rules such as it's wrong to steal. It's good to help others in need. Do unto others as you would have them do unto you.

In many ways, trying to live by these rules is the central part of life. The striving to acquire virtues like self-discipline and perseverance is perhaps the greatest challenge we all face. Life is, in essence, a moral and civic endeavor.

You don't have to be religious to have good moral values, but for many people, faith is the most vital part of morality. God anchors their sense of right and wrong. They believe that God has established the moral order of the universe. Faith lifts each person outside the self and inspires a larger sense of purpose.

None of us is born knowing right from wrong or having good moral values. These things have to be learned. So the task of each generation is to pass good values on to the next generation.

Conservatives believe that education is largely about the formation of good character. Young people acquire virtues like kindness and loyalty largely by practicing them until they become habits. They learn morality through the examples, expectations, and rules set by adults around them.

The family is the most important institution when it comes to forming character. The moral lessons parents teach make all the difference. That's a big reason conservatives are so concerned about the breakdown of the American family and the fact that so many children are growing up in homes without both a mother and a father.

Conservatives want the traditional institution of marriage to thrive because it helps keep families together. Strong marriages are not only good for men and women, but they're also the best way to raise children and give them solid values.

Community institutions play critical roles in teaching good moral values. Institutions like churches, synagogues, and other houses of worship. Schools. Neighborhoods. Volunteer groups such as the Boy Scouts and Girl Scouts, and the Boys and Girls Clubs of America.

In fact, the entire culture is involved in transmitting values from one generation to the next. That includes the popular culture—the movies we watch, the books we read, the advertisements we see on TV, the music we download. Some of the messages our popular culture sends—like do whatever makes you happy and it's fine to sleep around—are directly opposed to traditional values. They're the kind of values that can get us in trouble.

Why are traditional values important?

They're important because they are necessary for a good life. Human experience is very clear. When people ignore traditional values, when they abandon their responsibilities and act without integrity, they end up with empty, selfish, unhappy lives. When they hold to good moral values, their lives tend to be marked by happiness, fulfillment, accomplishment, and generosity.

Traditional values matter as much to society as they do to individuals. Russell Kirk, one of the most important conservative thinkers of the twentieth century, put it this way: "A society in which men and women are governed by belief in an enduring moral order, by a strong sense of right and wrong, by personal convictions about justice and honor, will be a good society—whatever political machinery it may utilize; while a society in which men and women are morally adrift, ignorant of norms, and intent chiefly upon gratification of appetites, will be a bad society—no matter how many people vote and no matter how liberal its formal constitution may be."[1]

The great Polish novelist Joseph Conrad, in one of his tales of the sea, described perfectly the man without virtues:

> They all knew him! He was the man that cannot steer, that
> cannot splice, that dodges the work on dark nights; that, aloft,
> holds on frantically with both arms and legs, and swears at
> the wind, the sleet, the darkness; the man who curses the sea
> while others work. The man who is the last out and the first in
> when all hands are called. The man who can't do most things
> and won't do the rest. The pet of philanthropists and self-
> seeking landlubbers. The sympathetic and deserving creature
> that knows all about his rights, but knows nothing of courage,
> of endurance, and of the unexpressed faith, of the unspoken
> loyalty that knits together a ship's company.[2]

The ancient Greek philosopher Aristotle pointed out that citizens are like sailors in a ship's crew. When sailors ignore their duties, the ship doesn't perform as well. When citizens ignore their duties, the ship of state doesn't sail quite as smoothly. Good, old-fashioned virtues make good sailors and good citizens. Among both, as Aristotle reminded us, "the salvation of the community is the common business of them all."[3]

What are "traditional American values"?

There are no particular values found only in America, but there is a broad set of ideals and beliefs traditionally associated with this country. Together, as a bundle, they make us who we are as a people.

Our fundamental values are written into founding documents like the Declaration of Independence and the Constitution. Abraham Lincoln once said that "my ancient faith teaches me that 'all men are created equal.'"[4] That "ancient faith" came to him from studying the ideals of the American founding and taking them to heart.

You can also find that "ancient faith" in great speeches and writings like Lincoln's Gettysburg Address and Martin Luther King Jr.'s "I Have a Dream" speech. Our finest values show up again and again in American history. Knowing that history puts the present in perspective and helps us know how to proceed.

Freedom of thought and speech. Equality before the law. The right to worship God as we please. A fair opportunity for all. The dignity of each individual. Government of the people and by the people. The right to one's own property. These are some of the values that lie at the American core.

American values also include certain habits and attitudes of citizens that make our country work—civic virtues, as they're called. Hard work. Individual initiative. Devotion to family. Respect for the law. Tolerance and appreciation for diversity. A spirit of commerce and free enterprise. Belief in the power of education. Responsibility for one's own actions and well-being.

All these and more make up traditional American values. You can no doubt think of others to add to the list. Conservatives believe it's a good collection of values, as good as any nation has ever known. It's a tradition worth standing up for.

Who's to say that one set of values is any better than another?

"What's true for one person may not be true for the next." "Who are we to impose our values on anyone else?" "If it makes you feel good, do it."

There's something very appealing about those kinds of statements. They have a freedom-loving, live-and-let-live ring to them. Saying them makes us feel nonjudgmental. And there's some truth to them. People are different, after all. They like different things and see the world in different ways.

Here's the problem. Some people take that kind of thinking too far. In their view, no one set of values is any better than another; different moral beliefs are all valid and equally true.

It's a philosophy called moral relativism. On the surface it may seem open minded, but it's deeply flawed thinking.

The fact is that some values and behaviors *are* better than others. For example, a man who tries to be a good father is acting better than a man who gets a woman pregnant and walks away without another thought.

Whether we want to admit it or not, we judge people by their moral values all the time, as we should. We don't choose people who cheat, lie, and steal as friends, for very good reason.

Moral relativism makes our eyesight fuzzy about what's really wrong and what's really right. When we take the attitude that there are no absolute moral standards, it's hard to tell the good and true from the false and shameful.

In 2014 the watchdog group Campus Reform asked students at Harvard University which is a greater threat to world peace: America or the terrorist organization ISIS. Some had clearly learned a "blame America first" lesson.

One answered, "In many ways I have to think it's America. . . . The amount of spending that America has [done] on causes of potential destruction in the world is really outlandish."

"American imperialism and our protection of oil interests in the Middle East are destabilizing the region and allowing groups like ISIS to gain power," another student said. "We are, at some level, the cause of it."

"As a Western civilization we're to blame for a lot of the problems that we're facing now," another said. "I don't think anyone would argue that we didn't create the problem of ISIS ourselves."[5]

This is the fruit of moral relativism—students who hold the United States in the same regard as a terrorist group that carries out beheadings, crucifixions, and mass murders of innocent people.

Moral relativism may allow us to tell ourselves that we're fair-minded, tolerant people. It's certainly much easier than calling out real wrongdoing. But it's a valueless way to see the world that leads to foolish thinking and turns a blind eye to evil.

Why do conservatives care about tradition?

Because there's much wisdom and truth to be found in tradition. It's civilization's way of transmitting the best values, thoughts, and achievements from generation to generation.

Traditional institutions like family and church are crucial for handing down good moral values. Written institutions like the US Constitution preserve freedom, equality, and other ideals.

Customs like Thanksgiving Day and rituals like the changing of the guard at the Tomb of the Unknown Soldier remind us of things worthwhile. They touch what Abraham Lincoln called "the mystic chords of memory"[6] that connect us to each other and to civilization's lasting vision.

"If I have seen further it is by standing on the shoulders of giants," Sir Isaac Newton wrote. We all stand on the shoulders of giants—the wisdom accumulated through centuries of human experience. We advance civilization by mastering that wisdom, adding a bit to it, and passing it on.

Conservatives appreciate the role of the past in shaping the present. That's one reason so many of them love history and its vast record of humanity's insights, trials, mistakes, and triumphs. Studying history helps us tell the difference between what's enduring and worthwhile and what's not. It can help us be better people.

"For in history you have a record of the infinite variety of human experience plainly set out for all to see," the ancient Roman historian Livy wrote, "and in that record you can find for yourself and your country both examples and warnings: fine things to take as models, base things, rotten through and through, to avoid."[7]

Tacitus, who followed in Livy's footsteps, added, "This I regard as history's highest function, to let no worthy action be uncommemorated, and to hold out the reprobation of posterity as a terror to evil words and deeds."[8]

Aren't "traditional values" really just racist, sexist, anti-gay attitudes?

No. That's an assumption liberals sometimes make. They'll say things like "Conservatives want to take us back to the time of segregation." If they really believe that, they have a profound misunderstanding of what conservatism is all about.

Conservatives don't want to go back fifty or a hundred or two hundred years. They fully understand that in a lot of ways, the "good old days" weren't very good for a lot of people.

That's true of even a few decades ago. Blacks lived with a set of traditions imposed on them that included staying out of "whites-only" restaurants, sitting in the back of buses, and far worse. Women, by age-old tradition, faced limited career choices. Gays risked ostracism and beatings. It should go without saying that it's good those norms are gone.

Conservatives understand that just because a certain value has been around for a long time doesn't make it right or good. Age doesn't necessarily determine something's worth. It has to be judged on its own merits. Values are good if they are good and bad if they are bad—regardless of whether they are new or old.

All over the world there are bad traditions and values that need to end. Slavery, for example, is an evil institution that has been around for thousands of years and still persists in many places in the world. There are still countries where ancient customs turn women into second-class citizens—forcing them into marriage, limiting their education, controlling their movement in public. Traditions like those are nothing more than human rights violations.

Societies can fall into bad conventions, just like people can fall into bad habits. Getting rid of them is one way civilization moves forward. Sometimes it takes a long time, just like getting rid of bad personal habits can take a while.

Conservatives aren't interested in perpetuating hurtful traditions. They want to preserve the ones that do good for people, ones that make lives fuller—like going to church and raising the flag on the Fourth of July. They want to end traditions that cause harm.

The story of Aeneas at the beginning of this chapter, when the Trojan hero carries his father and his household gods out of the burning city, helps us remember that carrying forward traditional values from one generation to the next is vital to civilization's success. But it's important to understand that conservatives are talking about carrying forward *good* traditions. The bad ones need to be left behind.

Isn't change the American way?

"Change is good." "You can't live in the past." "Go forward, not back."

Those are all, in a way, very American thoughts. The United States has always been about innovation and change. After all, we started with a revolution and became the first country created out of the belief that people should govern themselves. We're a nation of inventors. We've given the world airplanes, cell phones, the Internet, and rock and roll.

But it's important to recognize that sometimes "new and improved" turns out to be cheap and fleeting—like those miracle gadgets advertised on TV that end up in the junk closet. And what's old isn't always musty, stale, and stagnant. Often it's irreplaceable, like a solid old building knocked down to make way for a new one that turns out to have thin walls and a bad foundation.

Sometimes students jump to take new college classes like "Zombies in Movies 101." These classes sound fun, but they don't really teach much, and years later the students may well look back and think, *I wish I'd learned a little about Shakespeare or astronomy instead.*

Values shift, and the new ones may not be so good. How about a culture that values spending several hours a day surfing the Internet or watching TV instead of studying? Or one that decides it's acceptable to run up huge debts on credit cards instead of saving?

There is a part of human nature that gets bored unless it has something new and bright and shiny to occupy its attention. The writer C. S. Lewis called it "the horror of the Same Old Thing." The relentless desire for novelty can make an artist think, *Who cares what people painted five hundred years ago? If I make something startling and different, it's art.* (Never mind whether it takes any real talent and skill.) Or it can make a politician think, *The ideas of the founders are outdated. We need new principles now.*

Conservatives are always mindful that many traditions and values that have been around for a long time have lasted precisely because they do good. If we throw them out, there's a good chance we'll lose something precious and the replacement will be inferior.

It's tempting to always ask, "Is it new? Is it cool? Is it flashy?" But we shouldn't forget to ask, "Is it right? Is it good? Will it last?"

MARRIAGE *and* FAMILY

Eternal God, creator and preserver of all mankind, send thy blessing upon these thy servants, whom we bless in thy name. Enable them to perform through all their years the vows which they have made in thy presence.

May they seriously attend to the duties of the new relation into which they have now entered; that it may not be to them a state of temptation and discord, but of mutual love and peace. Grant them the virtues of trust and patience and undying affection. May they be blessings and comforts to each other, sharers of each other's joys and sorrows, loyal companions in the life and work of every day, and helpers, each to the other, in all the chances and changes of this mortal life.

—FROM A TRADITIONAL WEDDING SERVICE

WORDS LIKE THESE aren't as familiar to Americans as they once were. Even if they sound familiar, many people don't take them as seriously as their parents or grandparents did.

During the past several decades, family life in the United States has seen devastating changes. Here are some numbers that tell the story:

- More Americans are choosing not to get married. In 1960 about one in ten adults over the age of twenty-five had never married. By 2012 the number was one in five.[1]
- Far too many children are born to unmarried mothers. In 2010, 29 percent of children born to white, non-Hispanic mothers were born out of wedlock. For Hispanics, the rate was 53 percent. In the black community, 72 percent of births were to unmarried mothers.[2] Overall, four out of ten babies in America are born to unmarried women.[3]
- In 1970, 12 percent of children lived with a single parent. During the next four decades, the number more than doubled, to 27 percent. As many as half of all American children will spend some time living with just one parent.[4]

The late senator Daniel Patrick Moynihan of New York was once asked to name the biggest and most important change he had seen in his half century of public service. All over the North Atlantic world, he said, it was the coming apart of the family.

A few indicators are pointing in the right direction. For example, divorce rates and teen pregnancy rates in the United States have improved in recent years.

Overall, however, the traditional American family—one with a mother and father who are married and raising their children together—is in bad shape. This breakdown of the family is doing much damage to America.

Why has the traditional American family broken down?

There is no single cause of the breakdown of the traditional family. Shifts in people's values, habits, and attitudes have brought on changes.

One big cause is the modern emphasis on the self. Our culture is

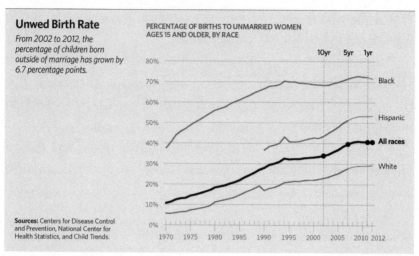

Unwed Birth Rate

From 2002 to 2012, the percentage of children born outside of marriage has grown by 6.7 percentage points.

PERCENTAGE OF BIRTHS TO UNMARRIED WOMEN AGES 15 AND OLDER, BY RACE

10yr   5yr   1yr

80%
70%   Black
60%
50%   Hispanic
40%   All races
30%   White
20%
10%
0%
1970 1975 1980 1985 1990 1995 2000 2005 2010 2012

Sources: Centers for Disease Control and Prevention, National Center for Health Statistics, and Child Trends.

Graph courtesy of The Heritage Foundation

full of messages like "Do your own thing," "Make your own rules," and "Don't let others define you." They're very American messages, in a way—ones about individualism and personal freedom. The problem is that people use that kind of thinking to justify selfish behavior like fathering children and then walking away from them.

Many people view sex as a "no-risk" activity they can enjoy without marriage. *As long as we use contraceptives or the morning-after pill,* they tell themselves, *there's nothing to worry about. Why tie ourselves down?*[5]

When they do get married, many view it not as a sacred obligation but as a contract, one that can always be broken. If they start to feel unhappy or bored, they just get out. Some marriages need to end, of course, especially in cases of spouse abuse. But far too many marriages end because people feel they have no moral duty to continue them and because they can easily obtain a divorce.

Living in an affluent society like the United States can put pressure on marriage. The more we have, the more we want, sometimes at the expense of relationships. Husbands and wives often spend more time at work and less time with family. If not enough attention is paid, marital bonds can come undone.

Meanwhile, many poor young women who get pregnant don't want to marry the fathers of their children because they don't trust them. They believe the men don't work enough or earn enough money or that they're too violent.[6]

All these factors and more have harmed the traditional family. Unfortunately, there are few signs that things will get better anytime soon.

What's so great about the traditional family?

The traditional family—a husband and wife living with their children—is vital to civilization's success. It is society's fundamental institution, the one where crucial lessons are taught.

Raising children is the family's most important job. Families supply the love, nurture, protection, and guidance that children can get nowhere else. Intellectual training begins in the home. For example, study after study tells us that young children become much better students when parents read aloud to them.[7]

Family is where the first and most important moral training takes place. Children aren't born knowing the difference between right and wrong. They have to learn how to be honest, brave, responsible, and kind. Teaching virtues is perhaps a parent's highest calling, and attention to virtues is one of the important ties that binds a family together.

"It is a characteristic of man that he alone has any sense of good and evil, of just and unjust, and the like," the ancient Greek philosopher Aristotle wrote, "and the association of living beings who have this sense makes a family."[8]

Parents teach crucial lessons in several ways. They teach by example. When children witness parents working hard, treating others kindly, and taking responsibility for their own actions, they are apt to behave the same way.

Parents teach by setting high expectations, establishing rules, and talking about right and wrong. Countless daily lessons—getting homework done on time, choosing the right friends, speaking respectfully to others—shape the kind of adults young people eventually become. When families fail to teach such lessons, young people's lives can go very wrong.

There is much evidence to show that, generally speaking, children who grow up without both a mother and a father in the home are more likely to struggle in many different ways. For example, children raised by single parents are not as likely to do well in school or get a college degree as children raised by married parents. They are more likely to engage in delinquent and illegal behavior. Daughters raised by single mothers are more likely to have sex and get pregnant while adolescents, and sons are twice as likely to spend time in jail. A child living with a single mother is four to five times as likely to be poor as a child raised by married parents.[9]

None of this means that a single mom or dad can't raise children well. Many do, and those children grow up to be fine, successful adults. But it does mean that it's much harder for one parent than it is for two. Single parents often find themselves spread too thin. Married parents can share responsibilities, so it's easier to spend time with children, set expectations, and enforce rules. The more two-parent families our country has, the better off it is.

It is impossible for government agencies or volunteer organizations to replace the family. They can provide some aid, such as financial assistance to struggling single moms or day care for children when no adult is at home. But government programs don't make good parents. When families fail, there really is no other institution capable of making up the difference.

Why are fathers important?

Fathers are important because children need them—badly. Boys and girls are better off with a devoted father in the home.

There are two different words meaning "father" in Latin. *Genitor* means a biological father. *Pater* means a father who takes responsibility. Unfortunately, there are far too many men who don't know or care what it means to be a *pater*.

In this country, about one-third of all children live apart from their fathers.[10] In some cases, it's unavoidable. But often young men are fathering children and then failing to meet their obligations. In many instances, they simply walk away and leave young mothers to struggle to raise their children alone.

Men and women are different creatures, and though their responsibilities as parents overlap, they offer different sorts of care. When fathers are absent from young people's lives, it's extremely difficult for others to replace them.

The time-honored responsibility of fathers is to protect their children from physical danger. Good fathers are sources of discipline and strength. Kids need to hear them say things like "If you cross that line, you'll have to deal with me" and "Real men do their duty."

Young boys tend to knock things over, smash things, climb as high as they can, get as dirty as they can. They need fathers to help keep their energy in check—to teach them it's not all right to push, hit, and grab.

As they grow older, boys need dads to help them channel their energy into studies, sports, and other activities. They need fathers to demonstrate how they should act when they grow up. That includes showing how good husbands treat their wives.

When boys grow up with committed fathers, they're more likely to do better in school, go on to college, stay out of trouble, and get a good job. Boys who grow up without fathers are more likely to wind up on the street or in jail, use alcohol, get into drugs, and be unemployed.[11]

For girls, good fathers provide security and protection—including protection from young men. They show what responsible, devoted manhood looks like. Girls who have warm, protective fathers are more likely to do better in school, be more assertive, and enjoy higher self-esteem. They are less likely to use drugs or alcohol, suffer from depression, abuse their bodies, or have a baby out of wedlock.[12]

Why should men and women get married when they can simply live together?

"Marriage is a relic of a day gone by." "We love each other; that's all that matters." "We don't need a ceremony or a piece of paper to be happy."

Those are the kinds of things people who live together without getting married often say. But marriage is much more than a certificate. It's a sacred and legal pledge to join a lasting, devoted union. It is—or should be—a solemn obligation.

Living together without marriage means living without that commitment. That might bring more freedom, but it also means that living together is less likely to be a stable, enduring relationship.

There are good practical reasons to get married. Married people tend to enjoy better physical health and psychological well-being. They're usually better off financially than unmarried people. Married couples report greater sexual satisfaction. They're likely to live longer.[13]

More important, there are powerful moral reasons to marry. Marriage is a shared moral endeavor. In healthy marriages, men and women try to improve themselves for the sake of their loved one. They strive to live up to the commitments made in wedding vows— to be faithful to each other, to love, honor, and take care of each other "in sickness and in health." Healthy marriages bring happiness, in part, because they make us better people.

Of course, marriages also make people happier because they often produce children. President Theodore Roosevelt once noted that there are many kinds of success in life worth having, but "for unflagging interest and enjoyment, a household of children, if things go reasonably well, certainly makes all other forms of success and achievement lose their importance by comparison."[14]

Marriage helps satisfy the deepest longing of the soul—the desire to love and be loved. Along with parenthood, having your heart braided to another is life's most joyful experience. "What greater thing is there for two human souls," the great writer George Eliot asked, "than to feel that they are joined for life—to strengthen each other in all labor, to rest on each other in all sorrow, to minister to each other in all pain, to be one with each other in silent unspeakable memories at the moment of the last parting?"[15]

For people of faith, marriage is sacred. The *Catechism of the Catholic Church* reminds us that "God himself is the author of marriage."[16] God created man and woman in his image, and their mutual love is an image of his absolute and unfailing love. This is the most profound aspect of marriage: it is a reflection of divine love.

Why are many conservatives against the idea of same-sex marriage?

Attitudes about same-sex marriage have changed amazingly fast in recent years. The country is divided about whether it should be legal, but a slight majority of Americans support the idea.[17]

Several courts have ruled in favor of same-sex marriage, and as this book was being written, it was legal in most states, with the issue headed to the US Supreme Court for a ruling on whether it is constitutional for states to ban it.

Many conservatives oppose same-sex marriage, but not all do. Conservatives of a libertarian bent are likely to think that government has no business telling people who they can and can't marry. Younger conservatives are more likely to support same-sex marriage than older conservatives. That's true of the population as a whole: younger Americans back same-sex marriage much more than older Americans.[18]

Conservatives who oppose same-sex marriage do so for a variety of reasons. Some believe homosexual behavior is immoral. For some, it's a matter of religious conviction. They believe that traditional marriage is a sacred institution established by God and that no one has a right to redefine it.

Some conservatives argue that creating children is central to the idea of marriage. It sets the union of man and woman apart from other relationships, which is why societies ancient and modern have given special status to heterosexual marriage.

Many conservatives also worry that redefining marriage as "whoever you love" opens the door to legal polygamy (marriage that includes more than two partners). Legal scholars have pointed out that if marriage is based solely on the principle of people loving each other, there is no rationale to deny three or four or five people who say they all love each other and want a group marriage.

Conservatives value tradition, so they're wary of changing such a fundamental institution. The traditional family is the best-proven setting for raising children. If we loosen standards to fit a "marriage is different for different people" attitude, many conservatives argue, there won't be much left of marriage at the end of the day. That will be bad for families, for children, and for society.

This nation has embarked on a large-scale social experiment with marriage. No one is sure how it will turn out. For conservatives who believe in the sanctity of traditional marriage, the challenge will be to navigate changes while maintaining their values. It won't be the first or last time they've faced such a challenge.

How can Americans put the institution of the family back together?

This is a hard question that Americans have been struggling with for quite some time. No one in Washington has come up with a good answer and, frankly, they're not likely to. These are not the kinds of problems that are really fixable from the halls of Congress or the White House.

In many respects, these problems are due to moral choices, such as the choice of a young man to father a baby he has no intention of raising. Or the choice of an unmarried woman to get pregnant when she has no intention of marrying the father. To fix things, the country's moral climate will have to change.

This means that attitudes and behaviors must change. That will take the effort of a great many people working together. It will take priests, ministers, rabbis, and other religious leaders. It will take principals, teachers, business leaders, Hollywood directors, actors, and sports figures. It will take government leaders, from the president on down. And a lot of moms, dads, and grandparents.

The messages will have to be loud and clear: men and women should be married before they start having babies. Raising children alone is a terrible struggle for most single mothers. Men who father children and then walk away from them are doing a terrible wrong. Men and women raising children together, as a family, is the right thing to do and the best thing for children. Marriage can lead to some of the greatest joys and deepest fulfillments people can know.

Can attitudes and values change? They can and do. For example, attitudes about racism have changed much for the better in the United States over the last several decades. Beliefs about the importance of marriage and family can improve too.

One thing is certain: messages matter. It makes a difference, for example, whether people get messages from television and music telling them that responsible teens wait to have sex and that good men raise their children—or whether they get messages saying that sleeping around is the norm and that everyone should live by his or her own rules.

In the end, the solution is up to individuals. Governments and other organizations can't make moral choices for people. They can give some help when needed. But it's the commitment of individuals that counts—individual mothers, fathers, and families nurturing their children.

FAITH *and* RELIGION

Our Father which art in heaven, we pray for all the people of our country, that we may learn to appreciate more the goodly heritage that is ours. We need to learn, in these challenging days, that to every right there is attached a duty and to every privilege an obligation. We believe that, in the eternal order of things, Thou hast so ordained it, and what Thou hast joined together let us not try to put asunder. Teach us what freedom is. May we all learn the lesson that it is not the right to do as we please, but the opportunity to please to do what is right. Above all, may we discover that wherever the Spirit of the Lord is, there is freedom. May we have that freedom now, in His presence here, to lead us and to help us keep this nation free. This we ask in Jesus' name. Amen.

—THE REVEREND PETER MARSHALL, CHAPLAIN OF THE UNITED STATES SENATE, 1947–1949

THIS PRAYER CONTAINS MUCH TO THINK ABOUT. The Reverend Peter Marshall opened the United States Senate's day with it on April 24, 1947, a time when humanity had just survived the catastrophe of World War II and faced the growing menace of communist totalitarianism. The prayer's wisdom is just as apt for the challenges of our day.

Not all conservatives are religious, but many are. Even the ones who are not religious tend to value the special role religion has always played in this country. Most conservatives believe that this country is a better, stronger place because of the American people's faith in God.

"Wherever the Spirit of the Lord is, there is freedom," the prayer says.[1] That belief has long been part of the American character. It's part of what makes the United States a great and good nation.

Is it true that this country's founding principles are rooted in the Christian and Jewish religions?

Yes. America's founding principles are rooted in several sources, from the writings of ancient Greek and Roman philosophers to the essays of Enlightenment figures such as John Locke. The Jewish and Christian faiths—sometimes called the "Judeo-Christian tradition"—were a vital source of ideals. They had an enormous influence on the founders' thinking.

Most of this country's founders were people of faith. They were overwhelmingly Christian, and in forging this nation, they looked to God. The first act of the Continental Congress meeting in Philadelphia in 1774 was to pray for wisdom. The members knelt with heads bowed as a clergyman read Psalm 35.[2] When George Washington became president in 1789, one of his first official acts was to ask the blessing of "the Great Author of every public and private good."[3]

The Bible was an indispensable source of instruction for the founders. In the eighteenth century, a time when books were still relatively scarce, if an American family owned one volume, it was likely to be the Bible. Those who could read knew whole passages by heart.

The founders naturally looked to the Bible for guiding principles. Professor Donald Lutz of the University of Houston examined the founders' writings and counted the times they cited authorities to bolster their arguments. Out of 3,154 citations, nearly 1,100 (34 percent) are to the Bible, far more than any other source of authority.[4]

Every American colonist who opened a Bible found this remarkable truth: God knows every individual's name, and he loves even the lowliest of his creatures. It was an idea that had taken root in the Jewish faith centuries earlier. The ancient Hebrew people had come to believe that each human being is important to God, that each matters equally in his eyes. In the days of Abraham and Isaac—a time of cultures that believed in many ruthless gods who killed men for sport—that was a radical thought.

Later religions, including Christianity, took up and spread this idea that all are equal in God's sight. In 1776 that deeply spiritual belief became the basis for the American ideal, spelled out in the Declaration of Independence, that "all men are created equal." Religion was a road map to the achievement of real equality.

The founders believed that all men are born with certain rights that are not subject to the whims of kings, such as the right to life and the right to control one's own property. These rights, the founders believed, came not from the minds of men or from governments but from God. As the Declaration famously put it, all men "are endowed by their Creator with certain unalienable Rights."

This firm belief in God-given rights runs throughout American history. President John F. Kennedy, in his 1961 inaugural address, reminded the nation that "the same revolutionary beliefs for which our forebears fought are still at issue around the globe—the belief that the rights of man come not from the generosity of the state, but from the hand of God."[5]

Why is freedom of religion crucial in America?

One of the "unalienable rights" named in the Declaration is the right to liberty. The founders believed that God creates all people to be free. He endows them with free will—the freedom to choose between right and wrong, to live a good life, to live to their fullest potential. Freedom, then, is a sacred gift. The founders were determined to set up a government that would not take it away from people, as so many kings and tyrants had done.

The founders realized that if American democracy was to work, it would need religion as an ally. Here's why. A government elected by the people relies on the people to make good decisions. Making good decisions takes wisdom and virtue. Therefore a successful democracy requires a citizenry of sound moral character. The founders believed that religion provides the best anchor for such national character.

This is not to say the founders believed that only religious individuals could possess good character. But they knew that religion helps people be good, and they were convinced that their experiment in self-government would fail without a religious population. George Washington put it this way: "Of all the dispositions and habits which lead to political prosperity, religion and morality are indispensable supports."[6]

Or, as John Adams wrote, "Our Constitution was made only for a moral and religious people. It is wholly inadequate to the government of any other."[7]

The founders made freedom of religion a fundamental principle for the new country. The First Amendment in the Bill of Rights says that "Congress shall make no law respecting an establishment of religion, or prohibiting the free exercise thereof." The founders decided not to establish a national church or to favor any particular religion, as England and other nations had done. In their view, that was the best way to keep religion and civil government from interfering with each other.

They wanted Americans to be a religious people, but they realized that a government that tried to force religion on citizens was asking for trouble. Faith is a matter of the heart and soul, and if worship is not given freely, it is not true faith. Liberty is the ground on which faith can grow.

James Madison put it this way: "The religion then of every man must be left to the conviction and conscience of every man; and it is the right of every man to exercise it as these may dictate. . . . It is the duty of every man to render to the Creator such homage and such only as he believes to be acceptable to him."[8]

For all of these reasons, religious liberty is a pillar of American freedom. It is the foundation of the American ideals of human equality, human dignity, and freedom of conscience. Take it away—take away a person's right to seek spiritual truth—and all other freedoms are at risk.

Why do some liberals want crosses and Christmas trees out of publicly owned places?

During the past several decades, the far left has tried to drive religion out of America's public square. Some on the left simply don't like religion and will do whatever they can to oppose it.

Others say we should ban displays of religion in publicly owned areas to preserve freedom. Radical secularists, as they're sometimes called, argue that to protect freedom, including the freedom of those who don't believe in God, government must have absolutely nothing to do with religion, and vice versa.

For example, secularists have tried in court to strike "under God" from the Pledge of Allegiance, remove religious symbols such as Nativity scenes and crosses from public parks, ban the display of the Ten Commandments in courthouses, stop legislatures and school boards from opening their sessions with prayers, stop public schools from beginning the day with a moment of silence for private prayer or meditation, ban Christian clubs from meeting on public school campuses, and stop ministers from praying at school graduation ceremonies.

Courts have issued conflicting rulings in these types of cases, which has created much confusion about what is legal. Fear of being politically incorrect has led to textbooks avoiding references to religion and Christmas trees being renamed "holiday trees."

Public schools and colleges are places where political correctness often thrives. Consider a few recent examples: In a Pennsylvania school, a teacher seized a little boy's Valentine's Day cards because they contained a message about Jesus.[9] In Montgomery County, Maryland, the school board voted to strip all references to religious holidays from the school calendar, including Christmas and Easter as well as Jewish holidays like Yom Kippur and Rosh Hashanah, and replace them with terms like "winter break" and "no school for students and teachers."[10]

Purdue University in Indiana stopped a donor from putting the word "God" on a plaque honoring his parents out of concern that it might offend someone.[11] The University of Wisconsin removed all Bibles from rooms in a lodge it owns "to make sure all guests are comfortable."[12]

Unfortunately, these kinds of incidents are not rare. Conservatives view them as badly misguided. The founders wrote the First Amendment to protect religion from government interference, not to discourage religious expression. Scrubbing religion from public places sends the message that religion does not deserve much respect. It sends a message that says, in effect, "Faith is not welcome here."

Why should religious symbols be displayed in public places when there are a lot of people who don't believe?

Most people want displays of religion like Nativity scenes or menorahs in public squares for good reasons. For most Americans, they are expressions of who we are, symbols of the deepest meanings of life. They remind us of our finest ideals and values. They celebrate the fact that we have freedom of religion.

We should always recognize that in a public setting, there are people of different beliefs. As Americans we respect each other's faiths, as well as the right of anyone who chooses not to believe in God. That means, for example, that public schools must not preach religion or force children to pray.

But there is a difference between a government that remains neutral about religion and a government that acts as though religion is a radioactive topic. There is a difference between being sensitive to other people's beliefs and being intolerant of people expressing their faith.

In this country, the danger is not that religions will go around forcing themselves on people. Americans have little tolerance for that. In the view of many conservatives, the greater danger is that the federal government will use its power to interfere with religion. The larger government gets, and the more control it seeks over people's lives, the larger the risk that it will restrict freedom of religion.

That's why conservatives stand up against the idea of driving faith out of the public square. As the Reverend Billy Graham once said, "The framers of our Constitution meant we were to have freedom *of* religion, not freedom *from* religion."

Aren't conservatives wrong to say this is a "Christian nation" when there are so many faiths here?

This is a "Christian nation" in that three out of four Americans identify themselves as Christians.[13] It is a "Judeo-Christian nation" in that its founding principles are rooted in Jewish and Christian religions, as discussed above. Those principles still make us who we are. But it is not a Christian nation in the sense that it was founded for Christians only or that the government favors Christianity over any other religion.

Scores of faiths, denominations, and creeds flourish here since immigrants from all over the world have brought their beliefs to America with them. Thanks to our principles of freedom, religious Americans are remarkably tolerant of others' faiths.

In many ways, the United States is a very religious country. Nine out of ten people say they believe in God.[14] About a third of Americans say they attend worship services weekly.[15] One-fifth of Americans are not affiliated with any religion.[16]

Does religion make America a better place?

Absolutely. Religion has been, on balance, an enormous force for good throughout the country's history. The longing to worship God freely gave the Pilgrims and other colonists the strength to endure

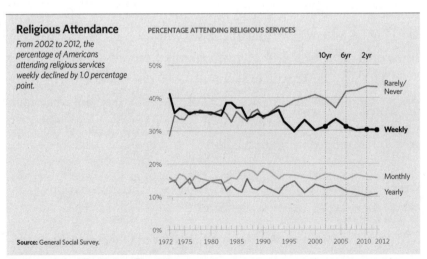

Graph courtesy of The Heritage Foundation

the long, hard task of settling in a new world. The movement to abolish slavery in the nineteenth century was spearheaded largely by ministers and others who believed that slavery was an offense to God. During the 1950s and 1960s, congregations led by ministers like Rev. Martin Luther King Jr. were at the forefront of the struggle for civil rights.

Take a look at almost any American community, and you'll see congregations doing good in all kinds of ways, from building houses for the poor to delivering meals to the elderly. (People who take a dim view of organized religion often don't realize just how much good churches and temples do, perhaps because they haven't made the effort to look.) Such work is a big reason why Americans give more than $100 billion a year—about a third of all their charitable giving—to religious institutions.[17]

Today we know that the founders were right in their belief that religion helps make people better citizens. For example, studies show that teens who take their religion seriously are less likely to use drugs and get involved in delinquent behavior like vandalism.[18]

Modern culture poses challenges for religion. We Americans live in a world of endless shopping opportunities and on-demand access to television, movies, and social media. In a society crowded with products and amusements, it's easy to neglect the spiritual side of life.

But as the founders knew, human beings are at their core moral and spiritual beings. For most people, faith is the anchor of morality. Religion helps us see life as something sacred and beyond the material. It helps us be honest, hardworking, responsible people. It prompts us to be less self-centered and to treat each other with kindness and decency. It offers a sense of greater purpose. Our lives become poorer when we neglect our spiritual nature.

All this is why conservatives believe that the more churches, synagogues, and other houses of worship flourish, the better off the country is. It's why conservatives stand up for religious traditions and why they believe it's important to remember where our blessings and freedoms come from. As George Washington wrote, "No People can be bound to acknowledge and adore the invisible hand, which conducts the Affairs of men more than the People of the United States."[19]

ABORTION

ABORTION IS THE FORCED ending of a pregnancy resulting in the death of the embryo or fetus—in other words, the death of a developing baby. Most conservatives share a deep concern about abortion. This chapter explains why.

The reality of abortion is harsh. It can be tough even to read about it. But reading in some detail is important because the language used in abortion debates—terms like "choice," "options," and "terminating a pregnancy"—often obscures what's actually happening. Here are some procedures used in abortion clinics.[1]

- During the first trimester of a woman's pregnancy, clinics often use a technique called suction aspiration. A suction tube with a sharp cutting edge is inserted into the mother's womb to pull and tear the baby's developing body from the wall of the uterus. It sucks the baby's remains along with blood and fluids into a collection bottle.

- RU-486, the "French abortion pill," is a chemical technique also used by abortion clinics during the first trimester. The pills block the action of progesterone, which is essential to maintaining the nurturing environment of the uterus, causing the baby to starve to death. A second drug, misoprostol, taken days later, stimulates powerful uterine contractions to expel the embryonic baby's remains. After taking the second drug, most women abort over the next few hours, but others may take days or weeks to abort.

- Dilation and Evacuation is a procedure used during the second and even third trimester. It often begins with the administration of a chemical agent to kill the developing child. The abortionist then uses a gripping tool called a tenaculum to grab, twist, and tear away parts of the baby's body until it is pulled from the womb, piece by piece. When the body is removed intact, perhaps with forceps grabbing the legs to pull out the entire body, the procedure is called Dilation and Extraction (or Intact Dilation and Evacuation). Because the child's skull has often hardened to bone, the abortionist must sometimes crush it before removal.

- Chemical abortion methods performed in the second or third trimester use drugs to trigger powerful, painful contractions that expel the child and placenta. As with surgical abortion, the abortionist may inject a chemical agent into the amniotic fluid, the umbilical cord, or into the fetus itself to make sure the child is dead before delivery.

Most people don't like to discuss the topic of abortion in this much detail. It makes them very uncomfortable, and when you know the procedures used, you can understand why. It's a deeply troubling experience involving untold loss and sorrow. But it's an issue that deserves careful thought.

Why do many Americans believe that abortion is deeply wrong?

Because they believe that abortions kill helpless unborn babies and often cause great pain to their mothers. And because this is a moral issue that tells us what kind of society we are. Do we have a culture that values human life or one that regards it as disposable?

This nation was founded on the idea that every individual life has value. The Declaration of Independence says, "We hold these truths to be self-evident, that all men are created equal, that they are endowed by their Creator with certain unalienable Rights, that among these are Life, Liberty and the pursuit of Happiness." That idea set us apart from regions of the world where rulers treated life as something cheap and expendable.

If we still believe that every life has value, then protecting life is our moral duty. And, conservatives believe, it should be the legal duty of our government.

There is a lot of talk in this country about saving things. Save the polar bears. Save the trees. Save the oceans. Conservatives want to remind the country about saving unborn children. Are they worth less than polar bears and trees?

Some people believe there is a category of unborn children definitely not worth saving—babies who are going to be born with mental or physical disabilities. They believe those babies should be aborted for their own good and the good of us all.

In 2014 Richard Dawkins, a famous evolutionary biologist, answered a woman who wrote on Twitter that she wouldn't know what to do if she were "pregnant with a kid with Down Syndrome." Dawkins tweeted, "Abort it and try again. It would be immoral to bring it into the world if you have the choice."[2]

Think about the cruelty of that statement for a minute. You may know or have met someone with Down syndrome. If so, you know that children with Down syndrome can live rewarding lives and bring much love, joy, and inspiration to others. Would you be willing to say, "You should never have been born" to such a person?

What other imperfections should disqualify someone from being born? A cleft palate? A missing limb? A heart defect? Who sets the standards about who lives and who dies?

Conservatives may be the most outspoken about abortion, but the truth is that just about everyone who thinks about the issue is deeply troubled over it. A solid majority of Americans say they oppose abortion in all or most cases.[3] Even abortion rights advocates sometimes speak of wanting the procedure to be "safe, legal, and rare." Why would they want it to be "rare" unless some part of them recognizes the tragedy involved?

What is *Roe v. Wade*?

Roe v. Wade is a 1973 ruling by the US Supreme Court that made abortion legal throughout the country. The court decided that every woman has a constitutional right to abortion.

Many people mistakenly believe that the Supreme Court made abortion legal only during the first trimester of pregnancy (the first through third months). In fact, the court created an almost unlimited right to abortion throughout a woman's entire pregnancy.

Here's how that works. The court ruled that until a child becomes viable (until it can live outside the womb), a woman can have an abortion for any reason she wants. After a fetus becomes viable, an abortion is still legal if a doctor says it's necessary to protect the mother's health.

But here's the catch. In a companion case called *Doe v. Bolton*, the court defined "health" as "all factors—physical, emotional, psychological, familial, and the woman's age—relevant to the well-being of the patient."[4] In other words, just about anything you can imagine that might affect someone's well-being in any way. For example, an abortion doctor could say that giving birth would cause a woman stress, and that would be enough to justify an abortion. In this way, the Supreme Court instituted a nationwide policy of access to abortion through all nine months of pregnancy.[5]

What's the result of *Roe v. Wade*? About a million abortions are performed in the United States every year. Thankfully, that number is down from a peak of 1.6 million in 1990. It is still a staggering, heartbreaking number. Well over fifty million abortions were performed in the four decades following the Supreme Court's ruling—about forty times the number of Americans lost in all of this nation's wars.[6]

Many conservatives believe *Roe v. Wade* is one of the worst rulings in Supreme Court history, wrong morally and wrong in legal reasoning. Nowhere does the Constitution describe a "right" to abortion. This is a case of judges inventing law rather than interpreting laws as written. The court should overturn its own ruling and let the people of each state decide this crucial issue through their legislatures.

What business do pro-lifers have telling women what they can do with their own bodies?

"Forcing a woman to have a child is morally wrong." "It's a private matter between a woman and her doctor." "Abortion is a woman's choice—it's her body."

These are arguments made by pro-choice advocates, as abortion rights supporters call themselves. They often say or imply that being against abortion is anti-woman. They'll even argue that the pro-life movement is part of a "war on women."

In truth, abortion is often dangerous for women's physical and psychological health.[7] Even if abortion leaves a woman unscarred, it's not simply a question of the woman "controlling her own body." There is another life involved, the life of the unborn child. If we believe in the value of human life, then we have to take that child into account as well.

"What you are calling a 'child' is not a human life," pro-choice advocates might argue. "It's not a person yet, so it's all right to abort it."

Recent advances in science have done much to demolish the argument that an unborn child is just a "blob of tissue." (For more on the scientific evidence, see the next question.) Even without science, common sense and ethics tell us that there's something wrong with the "it's not a human life" claim.

Before you were born, you were inside your mother's womb. You were less developed than you are now (just as an infant is less developed than a teenager), but you were you. There was nothing else in the womb that you swapped places with before birth. That was you. If you were not a human life, what in the world were you?

There is a reason mothers say, "I'm having a baby" when they're pregnant. They know they're carrying more than a "blob of tissue" inside. They're carrying exactly what they say: a baby.

Sometimes women face serious health concerns that require agonizing decisions about having an abortion. But the fact is that at least nine out of ten abortions in this country are elective procedures involving healthy women with healthy unborn babies. The most common reasons women give for having abortions are that they're "not ready" for a child or the "timing is wrong" or they "can't afford a baby now."[8]

The question is, are those good reasons for ending a life?

Women who decide against abortion need to hear a message from family, friends, and community that says, "You are not alone. We love you and will help you." Women who decide they cannot raise a child need to know there are many families in America who would love to adopt children.

This is not a "war on women" or anyone else. It's a matter of saving lives.

What does science have to say about the beginning of human life?

Thanks to advances in medical research, scientists know a lot about how a baby grows in the womb, and they're learning more every day. It's getting harder and harder for abortion supporters to say, "That's not a human life."

When a human sperm enters and joins a human ovum (egg), a living human embryo comes into being. From the very beginning, that embryo has a genetic composition that is distinctly human. When you were in your mother's womb, even at that early stage, your DNA contained the design that makes you unique—your blood type, your height, the color of your hair and eyes, the shape of your nose.

Human development proceeds at an amazingly fast rate. By about the sixth week of pregnancy, a baby's tiny heart has started to beat. By week seven, the baby's body is forming every organ he or she will need, including lungs, liver, kidneys, and intestines. Little arms and legs are starting to grow.

At eight weeks, a tiny face is appearing with the beginnings of two eyes, a nose, ears, and mouth. By week ten, connections are forming inside the brain. At twelve weeks, little teeth, fingers, and toes have formed.[9]

By twenty-two weeks of gestation, and possibly earlier, an unborn child can feel pain. This raises disturbing questions about what a baby experiences during an abortion.[10]

At twenty-three weeks, it's possible for a baby to survive outside the womb. More than 90 percent of babies born at twenty-seven to twenty-eight weeks in the United States survive a premature birth.[11]

People can always have political, philosophical, and religious debates about when life inside the womb becomes a "person" or "fully human." But search online for "sonogram of baby" and take a few minutes to look at some pictures. Or look at your own sonogram taken when you were in your mother's womb, if it's available. When you see those pictures, you realize that we're talking about human beings. The evidence is there before your eyes.

Those who are still not sure might want to ask themselves, *Isn't erring on the safe side the right thing to do? If we're not exactly sure when human life begins, shouldn't we take care to protect what may be life?*

Meanwhile, the scientific evidence keeps building. It deserves serious, thoughtful consideration.

How does abortion affect women?

Abortion can cause short-term and long-term physical problems for women. Possible short-term consequences include cervical lacerations, uterine perforations, bleeding, hemorrhage, serious infection, pain, and incomplete abortion. Possible long-term physical consequences include an increased risk of premature birth in future pregnancies.[12]

More damaging, perhaps, are the emotional and psychological suffering many women experience after an abortion, sometimes lasting for years. Abortion increases the risk of depression, anxiety, substance abuse, and suicidal thoughts and behaviors.[13]

Abortion rights supporters like to present abortion as an act of empowerment for women, something that allows them to control their own destinies. Liberal icon Gloria Steinem, who had an abortion at age twenty-two, once said, "Speaking for myself, I knew it was the first time I had taken responsibility for my own life. I wasn't going to let things happen to me. I was going to direct my life, and therefore it felt positive."[14]

A great many women who have had abortions do not share Ms. Steinem's feelings. They'll tell you they feel anything but positive about their experience. You can find their stories on the websites of organizations like the Silent No More Awareness Campaign (www.silentnomoreawareness.org), where thousands have written about the grief and sense of loss abortion can bring.

"My heart is still broken for what I did. It also is broken for the little life that I will never know this side of heaven."

"I am 65 years old now, but I will never forget that day. . . . I often think about her, what she would look like, her personality, and if we would be close. . . . If I could do it over, I would have kept her."

"I felt regret immediately. I look back and I don't know why I didn't go to my parents, a counselor, or someone from church. I don't know. Regret doesn't even begin to describe how terrible I felt."[15]

Some time ago one of this book's coauthors (Bennett) addressed a pro-life dinner and asked how many women there had had an abortion. About 80 percent raised their hands.

Those women became pro-life because they had learned something in a very personal, difficult way. They know the tragedy of abortion. They ask all of us to think very seriously about what it means and what's at stake.

K–12
EDUCATION

BELIEF IN THE POWER OF EDUCATION is a deeply rooted American value. Thomas Jefferson held that the "diffusion of knowledge among the people" was crucial to the American experiment. "No other sure foundation can be devised, for the preservation of freedom and happiness," he wrote.[1]

Jefferson and the other Founding Fathers emphasized the importance of skills like reading, writing, and calculating, as well as knowledge of subjects like history, geography, and science. They designed this country to be a place where a free people can use what they learn to make good, prosperous lives.

The founders knew that academics aren't all there is to education. Jefferson wrote that good schooling involves the improvement of one's "morals and faculties." That is, good schools teach character. They help students learn virtues like honesty, dedication, and respect.

The founders also understood that schools should help students learn the values, knowledge, and skills they need to become responsible Americans. The objects of education, Jefferson wrote, are "to instruct the mass of our citizens in . . . their rights, interests and duties, as men and citizens."[2] Good schools help make citizens who love their country, know about democratic ideals, and are not afraid to stand up for them. Otherwise, the American republic cannot survive.

Just about everyone has an opinion about education issues. That's partly because everyone has experience with school, either public school, private school, religious school, or home school. We've all run into great and not-so-great teachers, textbooks, and classes. We've formed ideas, based on firsthand knowledge, about what can be good and bad about an education.

We all have an ownership in American education, even after we graduate. Many of us have children or grandchildren who are in school, or we will someday. The health of our communities, our economy, and our whole country depends on our schools. Even the property values of our homes are tied to the reputation of nearby schools.

Given all this, it's easy to understand why education issues are often debated with passion. They should be. There is a lot at stake, and there is much work to be done.

Does America do a good job educating its students?

It would be a wonderful thing if most children in this great nation received great educations. Unfortunately, they don't.

- More than half of high school seniors taking the ACT or SAT don't have the skills they need to succeed in college.[3]
- According to national tests, about six in ten high school seniors can't read well. Three out of four seniors can't do math as well as they should.[4]

- On international tests, American fifteen-year-olds score below average in math, ranking behind many other countries, such as Japan, Korea, France, Poland, and Latvia. American students score only average in science and reading compared to other countries.[5]

The American education system faces serious, complex problems. If things don't improve, it could mean a dimmer future for the United States. Good jobs require good educations, and people who can barely read and write face a lifetime of financial struggle. The nation as a whole can't prosper as it has if other countries' citizens know more and can do more than we can.

Americans recognize this and have been trying to improve schools for more than three decades, with limited success. As the numbers above show, we have a long way to go.

Why is K–12 education in America mediocre?

Part of the problem—a big part, in fact—lies not with our schools but with events and trends taking place in our culture. The greatest threat to education is the breakdown of the American family. When large numbers of children grow up without fathers, or in households where single parents struggle to get through the day, or in households where adults aren't paying attention to their kids, schools feel it.

If you ask teachers what would most improve American education, you hear one answer over and over. They say, "We need more parental involvement."

You've likely been in classrooms where teachers have to deal with students who don't know how to behave because there is no one at home to teach them good habits. Or students who don't turn in homework because no one checked to make sure it was done. The less discipline and help kids get at home, the harder it is for schools to teach those students.

Another problem is all the distractions outside the classroom. American teens spend more than seven and a half hours a day watching TV, listening to music, social networking, surfing the web, and playing video games.[6] That compares to less than an hour a day doing homework.[7] Those numbers alone go a long way toward explaining things.

This isn't to say that schools are blameless. Too many have low academic standards. They set low expectations for students, and students learn to get by with little effort. Textbooks, tests, and assignments are watered down. Teachers let students make posters or draw pictures instead of writing papers.

In Japan, if a student doesn't do well in math, the answer is to do more math and work harder at it. Too often in America, students get away with saying, "My brain's just not that good at math. My grandfather wasn't good at math, my Aunt Gladys wasn't good at it—math just doesn't run in my family." The result: Japanese students are much better at math than American students.

Some schools don't focus enough on basic subjects. Students spend a lot of time learning to respect the environment but not so much time studying history. It comes as no surprise, then, when those students graduate without knowing what century the Civil War was fought in.

Won't spending more money on schools fix things?

"We need to pay teachers a lot more if we want better schools." "We need more computers in classrooms." "If Washington would spend more money on schools instead of tanks and missiles, education would be a lot better."

It's easy to think that if we just dumped more money into the system, things would improve. But we've learned in the last several decades that money alone is not the answer. More dollars do not guarantee better schools. Some schools spend a lot of money and get poor results. Other schools with fewer resources give children a fine education.

As a society, we invest enormous sums in education, and expenditures keep climbing. The United States spends an average of $13,500 per year on each public school student.[8] That's far more than most other countries spend.[9]

Most money spent on public schools comes from local and state taxes. Federal funds from Washington, DC, supply roughly one out of every ten dollars spent on education up through high school.[10]

As the graph below shows, since 1970 America has poured more and more money into educating students. Yet during that same period, test results have remained mostly flat.[11]

Good education is largely about effort and focusing on things that matter. Spending more money on schools won't help unless other changes happen.

Trends in Public Schooling since 1970

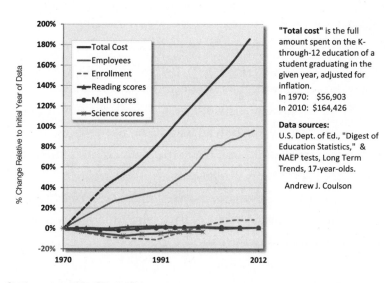

"**Total cost**" is the full amount spent on the K-through-12 education of a student graduating in the given year, adjusted for inflation.
In 1970: $56,903
In 2010: $164,426

Data sources:
U.S. Dept. of Ed., "Digest of Education Statistics," & NAEP tests, Long Term Trends, 17-year-olds.

   Andrew J. Coulson

Graph courtesy of the Cato Institute

Can't Washington fix schools for us?

There is an old story about the Greek mathematician Euclid, who taught geometry around 300 BC in Alexandria, Egypt. King Ptolemy heard of his fabulous calculations and asked for some instruction. Euclid started to explain some basic theorems, but the king soon interrupted. "I have little time," he said. "Is there no easier road to the mastery of this subject?" Euclid gently replied, "Sire, there is no royal road to geometry."

As in math, there is no royal road to education reform. There are no quick or easy answers. It's especially hard to fix American schools from Washington, DC.

Think about a class you took that wasn't particularly good. Maybe there were disruptive students in the room or an uninspiring teacher or a boring textbook. Whatever the problem, there is no lever a senator can pull or button the president can push to fix that class. Washington, DC, is simply too far removed.

Washington has tried. In 2001, during the administration of President George W. Bush, Congress passed the No Child Left Behind Act to improve student achievement. In 2009 President Barack Obama launched a program called Race to the Top to encourage reform. Between the two programs we've spent billions of dollars. It's hard to see that education has improved much, if at all.

Generally speaking, schools work best when local communities are in charge of them—not bureaucrats in faraway places. People who live near a particular school, who send their children there and see what kind of students it produces, know best what that school needs. A school in Boston might have very different problems from a school in Omaha or Los Angeles. That's why Americans have left most education decisions in the hands of local and state officials, not the federal government in Washington.

Fixing education is mostly a bottom-up, school-by-school process.

It starts with parents, teachers, and principals, and it takes the dedication of whole communities.

What makes schools get better?

Here are ten basic principles of education reform that conservatives adhere to:

- **Parents are the first and most important teachers.** Their efforts and expectations make all the difference. The more involved they are, the better their children's chances of getting a good education. When they remove themselves from the learning process, those chances plummet. Schools can't function well without parents' help. They can't replace the care a parent can offer.
- **Schools have to set high expectations for all students.** Here the old saying "Aim high" applies. Schools that maintain high standards get higher achievement from students. Schools that offer dumbed-down lessons and slipshod standards get little in return.

  Not all students have the same abilities, of course, so teachers must adapt lessons to appropriate levels. But all students should be challenged and expected to meet solid standards. Requiring any less is selling young people short.
- **Schools must be safe and orderly places.** Discipline and academic success go hand in hand. Where there is chaos, little learning occurs. In good schools the rules are clear— and enforced. The teacher is the moral authority in the classroom, with the responsibility to tell students how to behave. Parents and school officials back teachers up and make it clear to students that they must respect teachers' authority.

- **Schools should focus, above all, on academics.** Good schools are temples of learning. They present a clear, specific curriculum that states what students are expected to learn each year. That curriculum attends to the basics: English, history, math, science, and the arts. Most of the day is devoted to these core subjects. Good schools don't clutter the curriculum with so many other topics that the basics get pushed aside. They concentrate on essential skills: reading, writing, and speaking English well; analyzing and solving problems; thinking clearly and precisely.

- **Schools must help parents develop good character in students.** As the Reverend Martin Luther King Jr. reminded us, "We must remember that intelligence is not enough. Intelligence plus character—that is the goal of true education."[12] Good schools teach about right and wrong. They help young people acquire virtues such as self-discipline, diligence, perseverance, and honesty. Teachers cultivate these traits largely by helping students form good habits: getting to class on time, being thorough about assignments, speaking respectfully to others.

- **Knowledge is as important as skills.** Some schools are big on teaching "critical thinking" but not on mastering factual knowledge. They view memorizing facts as old-fashioned. But knowledge—knowing things—makes you smarter. You can't do much critical thinking about any topic without first knowing some things about it. There are some facts and ideas that all American students should know: what a right triangle is, where the Mississippi River is, what happened in 1776. Good schools have a clear vision of the knowledge they want to transmit.

- **Good schools teach civic virtues.** They help students learn to be responsible citizens. They help them learn to respect others and live up to obligations. They offer a good dose of American history, including events that tie us together as a people: the Constitutional Convention of 1787, the Battle of Gettysburg in 1863, the March on Washington in 1963. They teach the central principles that underlie American democracy. They acquaint students with their rights as well as their duties to this country.

· **Schools should be held accountable for results.** They should be judged by how much their students learn. For a long time, public schools resisted the idea of making sure that students meet certain standards. In recent years states have tried to correct this problem by coming up with standards in different subjects that schools must follow. The reform has been more successful in some places than others. There is still work to be done. But overall, it makes good sense that schools spell out exactly what they will teach students and then be held accountable for meeting those goals.

· **Good teachers should be rewarded.** Bad teachers should be given the opportunity to improve. If they don't get better, they should be dismissed. Most teachers are capable, dedicated professionals. But there are bad teachers as well. If you've had one, you've probably wondered, *Why don't they get rid of someone this bad?*

Unions such as the National Education Association have made it extremely difficult for principals to get those teachers out of classrooms. Sometimes it can take years of jumping through bureaucratic hoops. That's because the unions want to protect jobs. But putting jobs ahead of students' educations is wrong. In most professions, good work gets you rewarded, and bad work gets you a pink slip. Many schools would be better places with that approach.

- **Families should have the right to choose the schools their children attend.** In many places, the public school system assigns children to schools. This helps ensure that schools have a mix of students with different races and backgrounds, which is good. But there are downsides. Students sometimes get assigned to bad schools or schools that don't fit them well. That's wrong.

  Wealthy families get to choose their schools either by purchasing houses in neighborhoods with good public schools or by paying for good private schooling. Poor children, however, often find themselves trapped in bad schools. Many places have been offering more school choice in recent years, which is a good development. If parents are unhappy with a school, they should be able to take their children elsewhere.

Are some things more important to learn than others?

Conservatives believe that schools should transmit knowledge of important ideas, works, and principles from one generation to the next. Students should be exposed to great works of literature like *Hamlet* and *The Adventures of Huckleberry Finn*. They should know what the First Amendment means and what happened on D-Day. They should see images of great works of art like the *Mona Lisa* and hear great compositions like Beethoven's *Symphony No. 5*.

Such things are part of the culture all Americans have inherited—the "common culture," as it is sometimes called. These things are part of the glue that holds us together as a people. They help tell us who we are.

Most educators agree that it's important to teach about our common culture, but many schools do a poor job of it. For example, only about one in ten American high school seniors has a solid grasp of American history.[13] That goes a long way toward explaining why most American adults have a hard time answering questions like "What are the three branches of the US government?"[14]

Who decides what is most important to teach? Sometimes there are disagreements about particulars, but for the most part, it is a matter of consensus. Time is often the judge. The works of Socrates and Michelangelo, for example, have stood the test of time.

It is *not* a good idea for the federal government to dictate what American students should learn, for two reasons. First, if Washington was in charge, scores of different groups would lobby to influence the curriculum, and the result would most likely be a political mess. Second, there would be a terrible temptation for the federal government to influence people's lives by controlling what they learn. Far better to leave curricula up to the wisdom of parents, teachers, communities, and states across the country.

HIGHER
EDUCATION

*In the 2012 presidential race, according to Federal Election Commission data,
96 percent of all campaign contributions from Ivy League faculty and employees
went to Barack Obama.*

*Ninety-six percent. There was more disagreement among the old Soviet Politburo
than there is among Ivy League donors.*

*That statistic should give us pause—and I say that as someone who endorsed
President Obama for reelection—because let me tell you, neither party has a
monopoly on truth or God on its side. When 96 percent of Ivy League donors prefer
one candidate to another, you have to wonder whether students are being exposed to
the diversity of views that a great university should offer. . . .*

*Great universities must not become predictably partisan. And a liberal arts
education must not be an education in the art of liberalism. The role of universities
is not to promote an ideology. It is to provide scholars and students with a neutral*

forum for researching and debating issues—without tipping the scales in one direction, or repressing unpopular views.
—MICHAEL BLOOMBERG, FORMER MAYOR OF NEW YORK CITY, ADDRESSING THE GRADUATING CLASS OF HARVARD UNIVERSITY, MAY 29, 2014

AMERICA HAS THE FINEST SYSTEM of colleges and universities in world. It includes some of the best facilities, professors, and students anywhere. But it also has some big problems.

Colleges like to think of themselves as places where free speech, free debate, and free thought flourish. In fact, these days the opposite is often true. Many campuses are places where conservative ideas are reviled, shut out, and shouted down. Some professors go out of their way to sour young people on traditional American values like patriotism, trust in God, and enthusiasm for free enterprise.

There was a time when colleges played a role in sharpening not only the intellect but the moral sensibilities of students. On many campuses, senior year included a seminar with a name like "The Moral Life" taught by the college president, who was first and foremost a moral figure. Those days are long gone. Aside from freshmen orientations on issues like sexual assault, most universities steer clear of moral guidance.

American colleges claim that they give students good educations. Sometimes they do. But too often students graduate having learned little, or they don't graduate at all.

Students and their parents like to think that going to college is a good financial move. After all, college graduates generally make more money than people without a college diploma. But many college students graduate every year with huge student loan debts that take years to pay off, and many graduates struggle to find good jobs.

Are colleges biased?

Yes, they're among the most left-leaning places in the country. Not all are liberal. Some are not partisan one way or another, and there are even a handful of colleges out there (mainly Christian colleges) that are conservative.

But overall, the majority of public and private universities are ruled by leftist thought. Just about every liberal cause you can think of has strong support among college faculties, from promoting abortion rights to saving the world from climate change.

Departments that teach the humanities and social sciences—literature, philosophy, history, the arts, political science, women's studies, etc.—are most likely to be hotbeds of liberalism. Departments that teach science, mathematics, and engineering tend to be less biased, or at least less vocal about politics.

Surveys confirm that liberal professors dominate college faculties.[1] Consider, for example, the chart below based on data from the Higher Education Research Institute, which periodically surveys faculty members across the nation.[2]

Another study has found that in the humanities and social

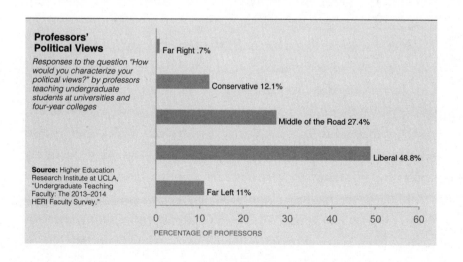

Professors' Political Views

Responses to the question "How would you characterize your political views?" by professors teaching undergraduate students at universities and four-year colleges

Far Right .7%

Conservative 12.1%

Middle of the Road 27.4%

Liberal 48.8%

Far Left 11%

Source: Higher Education Research Institute at UCLA, "Undergraduate Teaching Faculty: The 2013–2014 HERI Faculty Survey."

PERCENTAGE OF PROFESSORS

sciences, Democratic professors outnumber Republican professors by at least seven to one.[3] In some places, it's far worse than that. For example, surveys in the University of California system found the ratio of Democrats to Republicans among history professors to be 26:1 at UC–San Diego; at UC–Santa Barbara it was 28:1; at UC–Berkeley it was 31:1.[4]

US colleges love to boast about diversity on their campuses—diversity in race, gender, class, nationality, sexuality, and any other number of ways to group people. But when it comes to the political ideology of the faculty, they are anything but diversified.

The liberalizing of college faculties dates to the 1960s and 1970s, when liberal ideas heavily influenced the culture. Many conservatives believe that colleges discriminate against them when it comes to hiring faculty. The numbers suggest they are right.

Colleges are supposed to be places where ideas are shared and debated. Having faculty members who mostly think the same is not a recipe for stimulating minds. It is a recipe for conformity of thought.

Are conservative ideas tolerated on college campuses?

On some campuses, they aren't. Conservative ideas are mocked, shut down, or simply given a cold shoulder.

"It comes across that there only is a liberal campus," one student at Northeastern University in Boston told an ABC News reporter. "That's how I felt most of the way in college so far: that there is no room for conservatives there. . . . I know I have—or my friends have—spoken up about their views in political science classes and we get beaten down and laughed at." She added, "The faculty are—I don't want to say oppressive—but they are very not open to other views."[5]

In 2014, the College Republican National Committee began a Twitter campaign called #MyLiberalCampus, encouraging students to share their experiences with liberal bias. The tweets poured in.

"My professor called Republicans 'brain dead,'" one reported.

"My media ethics professor demanding that skeptics of global warming have no place in media coverage about the topic," another tweeted.

"A professor asked Republicans to raise our hands and said 'Oh Republicans, I wish that there were more of you . . . on Mars,'" another wrote.[6]

For commencement addresses, colleges love liberal speakers. In 2014 the Young America's Foundation analyzed who had been invited to address graduating seniors at the nation's top colleges. Liberal speakers outnumbered conservatives by nearly five to one.[7]

Some professors and students are so intolerant, they try to silence any voice they find objectionable. Protesters at several universities have managed to torpedo speaking invitations offered to conservatives.

For example, in 2014 a group of Rutgers University faculty and students raised a fuss when they learned that Condoleezza Rice, secretary of state under President George W. Bush, had been invited to give a commencement address. They disapproved of her role in the Iraq War. The protest caused Rice to withdraw as the speaker. She joined a long list of conservatives targeted by closed-minded liberals on campuses around the country.

Do colleges indoctrinate students with liberal ideas?

"Capitalism means exploitation and greed." "Racism is the fabric of the American flag." "We need more government to solve our problems."

Those are the kinds of messages colleges often indoctrinate students with. If you're a college student or are heading to college, chances are good that your campus will be a setting that tries to persuade young people that progressive thought is good and forward thinking and that conservative thought is foolish and even immoral.

You may well run across professors who use the classroom to promote their political views. You may even be unlucky enough to fall into the hands of a professor or two who, like one recorded at Eastern Connecticut State University, tell students that Republicans "want things to go back—not to 1955, but to 1855" and that conservatives are "racist, misogynist, money-grubbing people" who "do not want black people to vote, do not want Latinos to vote, do not want old people to vote, or young people to vote."[8]

You may find yourself sitting in classes taught through leftist perspectives, such as one that studies "environmental racism and ecological injustice in the United States." Or one that teaches "how social control dependent on power, privilege, and advantage continues to perpetuate sexism and racism."[9]

If your college is like most in the United States, you'll see professors driving cars with bumper stickers supporting liberal candidates. Eyes will roll at the mention of Fox News or Ronald Reagan. The faculty senate may pass resolutions supporting liberal policies. You'll see rallies supporting liberal causes like abortion rights and hear snickering comments about conservatives, especially conservative Christians.

Not all colleges are bastions of leftist thought, but many are, and their message to students is to think like a liberal.

Aren't professors smarter than the rest of us about how the world should work?

Surely someone who has a PhD has to know what he or she is talking about, right? No. That professor knows more than you about a highly specialized area, like medieval literature or existential philosophy. That does not mean his or her solutions to the world's problems are right.

More education does not equal more smarts about politics. Many professors are so insulated in the liberal bubble of academia that they have very little experience with ideas outside of it. They barely know the arguments on the conservative side!

Is it a good idea to challenge liberal professors? It depends on the professor. Many instructors welcome debate and engage with students in a good-spirited way. But some are narrow minded, rude, and petty about any dissent. You have to take measure of who you are dealing with.

If appropriate, by all means speak up and challenge the liberal line. A friendly debate of ideas is what college is supposed to be about. You don't want to get into the habit of being afraid to stand for your principles.

Debate will sharpen your mind and strengthen your arguments. It forces you to examine your beliefs carefully and articulate them clearly. It requires you to know what the other side is saying and how best to refute it.

Be courteous when challenging a professor or other students, even if they are not. Civility will help you make good points, think clearly, and have intelligent conversations.

At some point you may face a professor who penalizes dissent from liberal views. A UC–Santa Barbara student in a sociology course reported, "One of the questions on the multiple choice final for the class asked: 'What system is based on the division and exploitation of classes?' The answer to the question was capitalism, and in order to receive a good grade on the test I was forced to select that answer although I did not agree."[10] At times like that, it may be best to simply do the work required to get a good grade and move on.

Why study great Western thoughts, ideas, and works?

There was a time when American colleges made sure that students graduated with a solid grounding in the history and achievements of

Western civilization, including its literature, philosophy, religion, art, music, and scientific accomplishments. The curriculum examined great works and individuals, from ancient Greek and Jewish cultures up through modern times, including the history of the United States.

Think, for example, of the Bible, Homer, Beethoven, and Michelangelo. Or the Declaration of Independence and the Gettysburg Address. Through the study of great works, students learned how to think critically, write well, and apply lessons to new situations.

Practically all colleges have abandoned this idea of making sure that students receive a good classical education through a "core curriculum." Instead, they present students with catalogs full of choices that might include classes on the music of Lady Gaga or "Introduction to Popular TV and Movies."[11] At many universities students can graduate without taking a single course in American history or without ever having studied great works from the likes of Shakespeare or Leonardo da Vinci.[12]

There are several reasons why colleges no longer require studies in Western civilization. One is that schools have broadened what they teach to include topics that were once left out, such as the achievements of women, African Americans, and non-Western cultures. This inclusion is a good thing, but it often pushes aside classes on Western civilization.

Some liberal professors don't like the idea of focusing studies on Western civilization or any works produced by "dead, white males." In their view, the main legacy of the West is one of greed, oppression, racism, and exploitation.

They are wrong. The great works of Western civilization represent our culture's most magnificent thoughts and creations. They offer guidance when asking the great questions of life, questions such as, What is good? What should I hope for? How should I live? They teach us about virtues such as courage, honor, justice, and compassion.

Western civilization has shaped our country and our lives. It has given us our highest ideals. It has brought a long list of advances for humanity, from the scientific method to the world's most just and effective system of government, representative democracy.

All of our modern institutions are in some way the product of Western thought. How can we understand ourselves if we don't attempt to explore our past? As the Polish philosopher Leszek Kołakowski pointed out, in a culture in which your past is denied, you remain alien to yourself.

The story of the West is by no means perfect. Some of the chapters are dark, and they should be studied as well. But overall, the Western record stands extraordinarily high. Studying it tells us who we are and where we came from. Ignoring it makes for a poorer education.

Is it worth it to pay a lot of money for college?

This is a question that every student and parent (or anyone who is paying for a college education) should ask. It's the kind of question that good fiscal conservatives ask: Is the product worth the cost?

There has been a lot of negative news surrounding higher education lately. Many graduates are having a hard time finding good jobs. There are a lot of bitter young people out there who are waiting tables while they look for other employment. They are thinking, *I'll be paying off my college loans forever.*

It's fair to ask exactly what they got for all that tuition money. The ugly truth is that at many undergraduate colleges, not all that much learning goes on. Universities have dumbed down their standards and expectations. Many students spend much more time partying, hanging out, and playing video games than they do studying.[13]

A report from the National Association of Scholars states, "A considerable body of evidence now shows that recent college graduates are poorly educated . . . and are in general poorly prepared for the post-college workplace."[14]

Employers seem to agree. Eighty-four percent of employers rate college graduates as unprepared or only somewhat prepared to succeed in the workplace.[15]

Another problem is that some subjects may be a delight to study but don't make it easy to find jobs after college. That's especially true for majors like fine arts, anthropology, philosophy, and literature. Fair or not, they don't hold a lot of attraction for many employers.

But you don't have to despair about your higher education choices. Here are four questions to consider when thinking about going to college.

- **Who am I?** Many students go to college only because they think it's what's expected of them. They may go because all their friends are going. Or maybe they just want to party for four years.

  These are not the right motives for attending school. The right motives are ideas like wanting to get a good job someday (which doesn't always require having a college degree) and a desire to commit to serious learning.

  Many people never get completely honest with themselves about whether they are college-ready material or not. Many don't finish college because they discover they can't or don't want to do the work required. Make sure you're ready to knuckle down and complete that degree if you go. Your performance in high school will be a good indicator of your college readiness.

  If you don't think you're ready, consider going to community college to get into the rhythm of school in a less demanding setting. If you're not ready to attend college and do a lot of reading, writing, and lecture listening, vocational or trade school may be for you. There's also nothing wrong with just working for a while.

- **Where am I going?** Not all colleges are created equal. Some have very famous alumni, magnificent reputations, and world-class faculty. Others are institutions that very few people have heard of.

  In general, going to a really good school will give you a leg up when you go to look for a job. Employers will likely think you're smart if you've graduated from Duke, Rice, or the University of Michigan.

  That doesn't mean your future is dim if you don't go to a big-name school. Just make sure you don't pay a fortune to go somewhere that doesn't merit it. A degree from a top liberal arts or research school like Stanford, New York University, or Emory may be worth the cost. But an expensive private school that isn't so highly regarded may not.

  Go to Payscale.com and check out its helpful charts. They'll tell you the average cost of attendance at each school and the expected lifetime earnings of its graduates.

- **What am I going to study?** This is a very important question. You may feel more comfortable borrowing money for school if you study disciplines that are in high demand or pay well.

  These days, graduates who have studied STEM (science, technology, engineering, and math) subjects like petroleum engineering, computer science, and industrial chemistry generally make better salaries right out of school than liberal arts and social science majors (think history, philosophy, English, psychology, communications). Jobs in STEM fields are also usually easier to find.

  Of course, how much money you can make shouldn't be the main consideration in choosing a field of study. There are other questions to take into account, like "Will I be happy in that field?" and "Where do my talents and interests lie?"

  Still, it's smart to keep in mind that although there are

many wonderful benefits to studying subjects like foreign languages, art history, or sociology, those degrees may not get you a job as easily or earn you as much money (at least initially) as other degrees like nursing, accounting, and finance. Again, it might be useful to explore Payscale.com to see which majors pay best.

• **How much will I have to borrow?** College tuition has tripled over the last three decades, adjusted for inflation. The cost of one year at a private university equals, on average, more than half of an American family's income.[16] Students have been borrowing more and more to pay for college. The average debt load for seniors graduating in 2014 was about $33,000.[17] Some owe much more than that, even into the $100,000+ range.

Before you go to school, be sure you're making a smart financial choice. Will it be worth it to borrow $60,000 to study anthropology at an unknown school? Probably not. Will it be worth it to borrow $60,000 to study computer science at the University of Texas? Probably, since it's a well-known school that's relatively affordable offering a major that employers covet.

When thinking about how much to borrow, remember that one day your desires in life will change. Your deepest desire to study Shakespeare today might seem worth fulfilling at any price. But a few years down the line, when you are grabbed by the desire for a new car, a down payment on a home, or an engagement ring, you might regret borrowing a lot of money for a degree that hasn't amounted to a good return on investment.

It pays to be realistic about some hard-nosed questions: Will I get my money's worth at that school? How hard will it be to find a job with that major? How am I going to pay off my student loans? Would I be better off someplace more affordable?

These are difficult questions to ponder if you're in college or headed to college. The good news is that you *can* get a good education at most colleges if you choose courses wisely and study hard. If you do that, you'll be ahead of the game compared to most graduates.

CONCLUSION

We began this book by outlining several principles that conservatives hold, summarized by the acronym FLINT—Free enterprise, Limited government, Individual liberty, National defense, and Traditional values. All of the issues discussed in these pages touch on one or more of those principles. Taken together, they help inform a conservative vision for this country.

The United States was founded on these principles, and its strength still lies in them. Each generation has the responsibility to explain them to the next, to help younger Americans understand why they are good and what they have meant to the world. That conversation helps ensure a promising future. It helps keep America strong.

What kind of country do conservatives want America to be?

Conservatives understand that the culture shapes and reflects people's values. They want American culture to be one that helps transmit good values from one generation to another—virtues like honesty, hard work, and generosity of spirit.

Families are crucial to the task of transmitting such virtues. Conservatives want America to be a place where the institution of marriage is strong. They want children to have, whenever possible, the benefit of growing up with a mother and father in the home. When that's not possible, they want children to have strong adult role models to help nurture and teach them.

Families need the help of the entire culture. The conservative vision of America is one in which all the "little platoons" of society—churches, synagogues, neighborhood associations, schools, businesses, and volunteer groups—work to make communities good, healthy places to live.

Religion plays a special role in that mix. Conservatives are strong defenders of people's right to worship—or not to worship—as they see fit. Faith is a matter of the heart and should never be forced or required of anyone. But conservatives also believe that religion helps make America a good place. They want the United States to continue to be a nation where faith in God is strong and where churches and other houses of worship flourish.

Conservatives want schools to be places with high expectations that focus on academics and help parents develop good character in students. Schools should teach the knowledge, skills, and values that enable young Americans to become good citizens and prosper in a free economy.

That includes teaching about the principles upon which this country was founded, ideals such as that all people are created equal and that all have the right to think and speak freely. It includes an honest teaching about America's past and an explanation that, despite its flaws, this nation is one of the greatest nations in history. Conservatives want schools to help raise patriots who are grateful to live in this country and who want to improve it.

Conservatives believe that our laws should be color blind. They want the United States to be known as the best place on earth to be a minority. They believe we should continue our long tradition of welcoming immigrants to our shores but that our borders must be safe and secure and that immigrants should come here legally, respecting our laws.

One measure of any society is how well it protects its most vulnerable members. Conservatives believe society should protect the lives of unborn babies—the most vulnerable and innocent among us.

Conservatives recognize that free enterprise is the engine that has made the United States an economic powerhouse. They want a strong American free enterprise system that offers a good standard of living and economic opportunity to the most people.

Conservatives envision a federal government equal to the task of serving a great and powerful nation. That means one that protects citizens' liberties and rights but does not try to run their lives, one that helps tackle big issues but does not claim to be the solution to every problem that comes along. It means a national government that doesn't hog all the power and that respects people's right to govern themselves through state and local governments.

There are some things that the federal government in Washington, DC, must do. One of them is to defend the country from enemies. Conservatives want America to maintain the strongest military in the world to protect our freedom and to stand up to tyranny when necessary.

We all have an obligation to help those in true need, especially here in the most prosperous nation on earth. Conservatives recognize that government plays an important role in providing that help, but also that there is only so much government can do.

We all have an obligation for good stewardship of the earth. Conservatives expect government to help protect the environment. They also expect government to recognize that good stewardship involves putting the earth's resources to work in sensible ways that benefit people.

Conservatives expect government to handle these tasks with smart, efficient programs, not programs that just throw money at problems and waste taxpayer dollars. Government should operate under the same financial reality that American families have to live by. It should balance its budget, spending only as much money as it receives.

American democracy is based on the idea of personal responsibility—a free people making sound decisions for themselves, both in the voting booth and in everyday life. Conservatives want a country where citizens know that liberty comes with responsibility, where people respect the rights of others, obey the law, and are accountable for their actions.

Conservatives don't buy into grand promises that government can make sweeping changes that make people's problems go away. But they want a good society and sound government. They believe that as long as America remembers its founding principles and strives to live up to them, it can be a great country.

ACKNOWLEDGMENTS

THIS BOOK WAS WRITTEN with the help of a very smart, energetic group who gave generously of their time and expertise.

For reading, commenting, and correcting, we'd like to thank Steven Hayward, Seth Leibsohn, Susan Muskett, Penny Nance, Dr. Randall K. O'Bannon, James Pethokoukis, and Jessica Prol. They are all people who have a keen grasp of some crucial issues facing our country. They set us right more than once.

Chris Beach and David Wilezol gave invaluable help in several ways, from advising about source material to commenting on draft chapters. They are both wise beyond their years.

We owe a special thanks to Peter Wehner. Before writing a single word, we turned to Pete for guidance. He later read every paragraph of every page and gave us his insights. His prudence and judgment made it a better book.

Noreen Burns helped keep everything on track, as she always does. Her ability to fix, arrange, find, and plan all at once is absolutely amazing.

Christian Pinkston helped get the idea of this book going early on. We are grateful for his very considerable talent, skill, and friendship.

The Heritage Foundation, the Cato Institute, and the Competitive

Enterprise Institute kindly gave permission to reprint graphs that do a brilliant job of illustrating some truths and trends. We are grateful to have been able to draw on the work of Romina Boccia, Andrew J. Coulson, Clyde Wayne Crews, Rea Hederman, Jennifer Marshall, and others for these images.

Molly Cribb and Louise Franke helped make sure this book is a good fit for young Americans. They are part of an impressive rising generation that gives us hope that this country's best days are ahead.

Bob Barnett gave his always-excellent counsel. The world of writing and publishing runs more smoothly because of Bob.

Ron Beers, Jon Farrar, Jonathan Schindler, and the entire team at Tyndale House have been wonderful to work with. They know what they are doing, and they do it with great warmth and humility.

Our efforts benefited immensely from the candor, intelligence, and goodwill of callers to *Bill Bennett's Morning in America* radio show. John Adams believed that for America to succeed, its citizens must possess "the ideas of right and the sensations of freedom." Adams would have loved the *Morning in America* audience. Both of this book's authors have learned from listening to them.

Finally, we give thanks to and for our wives, sons, and daughters: Elayne, John, and Joe Bennett and Kirsten, Molly, and Sarah Cribb. In the riches of family, we are blessed beyond all deserving.

NOTES

INTRODUCTION
1. Lydia Saad, "U.S. Liberals at Record 24%, but Still Trail Conservatives," Gallup, January 9, 2015, http://www.gallup.com/poll/180452/liberals-record-trail -conservatives.aspx.
2. Debra Saunders, "Angry White Men—aka Journalists," Real Clear Politics, May 13, 2014, http://www.realclearpolitics.com/articles/2014/05/13/angry_white_men_--_ aka_journalists_122614.html.
3. "Media Bias 101: What Journalists Really Think—and What the Public Thinks about Them," Media Research Center, updated May 19, 2014, http://www.mrc.org/media -bias-101/media-bias-101-what-journalists-really-think-and-what-public-thinks -about-them.
4. Ruth R. Wisse, "The Closing of the Collegiate Mind," *Wall Street Journal*, May 11, 2014, http://www.wsj.com/news/articles/SB10001424052702303701304579550340 0222538088.
5. Kendall Breitman, "Obama to GOP: Stop Hating," *Politico*, July 30, 2014, http:// www.politico.com/story/2014/07/obama-gop-stop-hating-109543.html.

CONSERVATIVE PRINCIPLES: AN OVERVIEW
1. Abigail Adams, letter to John Adams, November 27, 1775.
2. Jeanine Cali, "Frequent Reference Question: How Many Federal Laws Are There?" *In Custodia Legis* (blog of the Law Library of Congress), March 12, 2013, http://blogs .loc.gov/law/2013/03/frequent-reference-question-how-many-federal-laws-are-there/.
3. Debt estimate figures from US Debt Clock.org, available at http://www.usdebtclock .org/ (accessed January 23, 2015).
4. Aristotle, *Politics*, Book VI, Part IV.
5. Rebecca Riffkin, "Public Faith in Congress Falls Again, Hits Historic Low," Gallup, June 19, 2014, http://www.gallup.com/poll/171710/public-faith-congress-falls-again -hits-historic-low.aspx.

6. John Stuart Mill, "The Contest in America," *Fraser's Magazine*, February 1862.
7. Proverbs 8:12.

THE AMERICAN RECORD
1. Justin Gillis, "Norman Borlaug, Plant Scientist Who Fought Famine, Dies at 95," *New York Times*, September 13, 2009, available at http://www.nytimes.com/2009/09/14/business/energy-environment/14borlaug.html; Gregg Easterbrook, "The Man Who Defused the 'Population Bomb,'" *Wall Street Journal*, September 16, 2009, http://online.wsj.com/news/articles/SB1000142405297020391730457441138266924044?mg=reno64-wsj&url=http%3A%2F%2Fonline.wsj.com%2Farticle%2FSB10001424052970203917304574411382676924044.html.
2. Easterbrook, "The Man Who Defused the 'Population Bomb.'"
3. James Madison, *Federalist Papers*, no. 14, November 30, 1787.
4. General Colin Powell (remarks at the World Economic Forum, January 26, 2003).
5. Gordon Sinclair (radio broadcast, June 5, 1973), http://www.broadcasting-history.ca/index3.html?url=http%3A//www.broadcasting-history.ca/news/unique/am_text.html.
6. William J. Bennett and John T. E. Cribb, *The American Patriot's Almanac* (Nashville: Thomas Nelson, 2010), xvi.
7. John Winthrop, "A Model of Christian Charity" (sermon, written on board the *Arbella*, 1630).
8. John F. Kennedy (undelivered remarks to the Dallas Citizens Council, Trade Mart, Dallas, Texas, November 22, 1963).
9. Abraham Lincoln (annual message to Congress, December 1, 1862).

FREE ENTERPRISE
1. Tas Anjarwalla, "Inventor of Cell Phone: We Knew Someday Everybody Would Have One," edited transcript of interview with Martin Cooper, CNN, July 9, 2010, http://www.cnn.com/2010/TECH/mobile/07/09/cooper.cell.phone.inventor/index.html?hpt=Sbin.
2. M. Dorothy George, *London Life in the Eighteenth Century* (Academy Chicago Publishers, 1985), 42.
3. Peter Wehner and Arthur C. Brooks, *Wealth and Justice: The Morality of Democratic Capitalism* (Washington, DC: AEI Press, 2011), 12–14.
4. Charles Dickens, *Hard Times*, chapter V.
5. Wehner and Brooks, *Wealth and Justice*, 38.
6. Ken Sweet, "Median CEO Pay Rose to More Than $10 Million Last Year," Associated Press, May 27, 2014, http://www.huffingtonpost.com/2014/05/27/median-ceo-pay-10-million-_n_5395443.html.
7. Wehner and Brooks, *Wealth and Justice*, 24–25.
8. 2 Corinthians 9:7.
9. Abraham Lincoln (speech, Kalamazoo, Michigan, August 27, 1856).
10. Calvin Coolidge, "Speech on the Occasion of the One Hundred and Fiftieth Anniversary of the Declaration of Independence" (Philadelphia, July 5, 1926).
11. Pope John Paul II, *Sollicitudo Rei Socialis*, December 30, 1987, http://www.vatican.va/holy_father/john_paul_ii/encyclicals/documents/hf_jp-ii_enc_30121987_sollicitudo-rei-socialis_en.html.

12. Michael J. Totten, "The Last Communist City," *City Journal*, Spring 2014, http://www.city-journal.org/2014/24_2_havana.html.

EQUALITY AND OPPORTUNITY

1. See, for example, "Social Injustice," Snopes.com, accessed August 12, 2014, http://www.snopes.com/college/exam/socialism.asp.
2. Proverbs 14:21, RSV.
3. John Locke, *Second Treatise of Government* (1690), chapter VII, sec. 87.
4. Michael Burlingame, *Abraham Lincoln: A Life,* vol. 1 (Baltimore: Johns Hopkins University Press, 2008), 567.
5. Robert Rector, "Self-Sufficiency Rate Stagnates, Welfare State Grows," in the 2014 Index of Culture and Opportunity, edited by Jennifer A. Marshall and Rea S. Hederman Jr. (The Heritage Foundation, 2014), 47, http://index.heritage.org/culture/self-sufficiency/.
6. Ron Haskins, "Getting Ahead in America," *National Affairs*, no. 1 (Fall 2009): 48, http://www.nationalaffairs.com/publications/detail/getting-ahead-in-america.

ENERGY AND THE ENVIRONMENT

1. "1970: Walter Cronkite Reports on First Earth Day," video of CBS News Special "Earth Day: A Question of Survival," April 22, 1970, http://www.cbsnews.com/videos/1970-walter-cronkite-reports-on-first-earth-day/.
2. The original *Washington Post* headline contained a typo. "Herald" was misprinted as "held."
3. Mark J. Perry, "18 Spectacularly Wrong Apocalyptic Predictions Made around the Time of the First Earth Day in 1970, Expect More This Year," *AEIdeas* (blog), The American Enterprise Institute, April 21, 2014, http://www.aei-ideas.org/2014/04/18-spectacularly-wrong-apocalyptic-predictions-made-around-the-time-of-the-first-earth-day-in-1970-expect-more-this-year/.
4. Ibid.
5. "Energy Overview," The World Bank, http://www.worldbank.org/en/topic/energy/overview#1.
6. US Environmental Protection Agency, Office of Mobile Resources, "Automobile Emissions: An Overview," Fact Sheet OMS-5 (August 1994), 4, http://www.epa.gov/otaq/consumer/05-autos.pdf.
7. Grant Smith, "U.S. Seen as Biggest Oil Producer after Overtaking Saudi," Bloomberg News, July 4, 2014, http://www.bloomberg.com/news/2014-07-04/u-s-seen-as-biggest-oil-producer-after-overtaking-saudi.html.
8. Ezra Klein, "Al Gore Explains Why He's Optimistic about Stopping Global Warming," *Washington Post Wonkblog*, August 21, 2013, http://www.washingtonpost.com/blogs/wonkblog/wp/2013/08/21/al-gore-explains-why-hes-optimistic-about-stopping-global-warming/.
9. Steven Hayward, "Climatistas Don Their Brownshirts," *Power Line* (blog), September 23, 2014, http://www.powerlineblog.com/archives/2014/09/climatistas-don-their-brownshirts.php.
10. Joseph Bast and Roy Spencer, "The Myth of the Climate Change '97%,'" *Wall Street Journal*, May 26, 2014, http://online.wsj.com/news/articles/SB10001424052702303480304579578462813553136.

11. Lianne M. Lefsrud and Renate E. Meyer, "Science or Science Fiction? Professionals' Discursive Construction of Climate Change," *Organization Studies* 33, no. 11 (November 2012): 1477–1506, http://oss.sagepub.com/content/33/11/1477.full.

12. Steven E. Koonin, "Climate Science Is Not Settled," *Wall Street Journal*, September 19, 2014, http://online.wsj.com/articles/climate-science-is-not-settled-1411143565.

13. Ibid.

14. Ibid.

15. Paul Bedard, "Reporters Told to Stop Interviewing 'Irrelevant' Climate Change Critics," *Washington Examiner*, February 10, 2015, http://www.washingtonexaminer.com /reporters-told-to-stop-interviewing-irrelevant-climate-change-critics/article/2560039.

16. John Hinderaker, "Was 2014 Really the Warmest Year Ever?" *Power Line* (blog), January 16, 2015, http://www.powerlineblog.com/archives/2015/01/was-2014 -really-the-warmest-year-ever.php.

17. Richard W. Rahn, "RAHN: The Global-Warming Apocalypses That Didn't Happen," *Washington Times*, April 21, 2014, http://www.washingtontimes.com/news/2014 /apr/21/rahn-the-world-did-not-end/.

18. John Feffer, "Crapshoot in Copenhagen," Foreign Policy in Focus, December 8, 2009, http://fpif.org/crapshoot_in_copenhagen/.

LIMITED GOVERNMENT

1. Paul Ryan, *The Way Forward* (New York: Twelve, 2014), 153–54.

2. Ronald Reagan, "Farewell Address to the Nation" (Washington, DC, January 11, 1989).

3. Ron Chernow, *Alexander Hamilton* (New York: The Penguin Press, 2005), 471.

4. Bernard Bailyn, *The Ideological Origins of the American Revolution* (Cambridge, MA: Harvard University Press, 1992), 60.

5. Thomas Jefferson, letter to Edward Carrington, May 27, 1788.

6. Abraham Lincoln, "Fragment on Government," in Roy P. Basler, ed., *The Collected Works of Abraham Lincoln*, vol. II (New Brunswick, NJ: Rutgers University Press, 1953), 220.

7. US Office of Personnel Management, "Historical Federal Workforce Tables: Total Government Employment Since 1962," http://www.opm.gov/policy-data-oversight /data-analysis-documentation/federal-employment-reports/historical-tables/total -government-employment-since-1962/.

8. United States Census Bureau, "2012 Census of Governments: Employment Summary Report," March 6, 2014, https://www.census.gov/govs/apes/.

9. Clyde Wayne Crews, *Ten Thousand Commandments: An Annual Snapshot of the Federal Regulatory State* (Competitive Enterprise Institute, 2014), 2, http://cei.org/studies /ten-thousand-commandments-2014.

10. Ibid.

11. Woodrow Wilson, *The State* (Boston: D.C. Heath, 1889), 651.

12. Lyndon B. Johnson, "The Great Society" (speech, University of Michigan, Ann Arbor, May 22, 1964).

13. Romina Boccia, "Federal Spending by the Numbers, 2014: Government Spending Trends in Graphics, Tables, and Key Points (Including 51 Examples of Government Waste)," The Heritage Foundation, December 8, 2014, http://www.heritage.org /research/reports/2014/12/federal-spending-by-the-numbers-2014.

14. Debt estimate figures from US Debt Clock.org, http://www.usdebtclock.org/ (accessed February 24, 2014).
15. Crews, *Ten Thousand Commandments*, 2, 12.
16. The Associated Press, "Social Security's $300 Million IT Project Doesn't Work," July 24, 2014, http://www.dailyfinance.com/2014/07/24/social-security-computer-woes/.
17. Romina Boccia and Matthew Sabas, "Booze, Pole Dancing, and Luxurious Hotels: Top 10 Examples of Government Waste in 2013," *The Daily Signal*, December 30, 2013, http://dailysignal.com/2013/12/30/mb-1230-booze-pole-dancing-luxurious -hotels-top-10-examples-government-waste-2013/.
18. Merrill Matthews, "Government Programs Have Become One Big Scammer Fraud Fest," *Forbes*, January 13, 2014, http://www.forbes.com/sites/merrillmatthews/2014 /01/13/government-programs-have-become-one-big-scammer-fraud-fest/.
19. Michael Puma et al., "Third Grade Follow-up to the Head Start Impact Study Final Report," OPRE Report #2012-45 (Washington, DC: Office of Planning, Research and Evaluation, Administration for Children and Families, U.S. Department of Health and Human Services, October 2012), http://www.acf.hhs.gov/programs /opre/resource/third-grade-follow-up-to-the-head-start-impact-study-final-report.
20. George McGovern, "A Politician's Dream Is a Businessman's Nightmare," *Wall Street Journal*, June 1, 1992, http://digital.library.ucla.edu/websites/2008_993_056/Politician _Dream.htm.
21. Pew Research Center, "Majority Says the Federal Government Threatens Their Personal Rights," January 31, 2013, http://www.people-press.org/2013/01/31 /majority-says-the-federal-government-threatens-their-personal-rights/.
22. Ryan, *The Way Forward*, 189.
23. Alexis de Tocqueville, *Democracy in America*, vol. 2, part 2, ch. 5.
24. Yuval Levin, "A Conservative Governing Vision," in *Room to Grow* (YG Network, 2014), 15–21, http://ygnetwork.org/roomtogrow/.
25. de Tocqueville, *Democracy in America*, vol. 2, part 2, ch. 7.

THE WELFARE STATE

1. Lyndon B. Johnson, "The Great Society" (speech, University of Michigan, Ann Arbor, May 22, 1964).
2. Nicholas Eberstadt, "Are Entitlements Corrupting Us? Yes, American Character Is at Stake," *Wall Street Journal*, August 31, 2012, http://online.wsj.com/news/articles/SB1 0000872396390444914904577619671931313542.
3. Ibid.
4. Ibid.
5. Paul Ryan, *The Way Forward* (New York: Twelve, 2014), 177.
6. Lyndon B. Johnson, "Annual Message to the Congress on the State of the Union" (speech, Washington, DC, January 8, 1964).
7. Robert Rector, "Self-Sufficiency Rate Stagnates, Welfare State Grows," in *2014 Index of Culture and Opportunity*, ed. Jennifer A. Marshall and Rea S. Hederman Jr. (The Heritage Foundation, 2014), 47–48, http://index.heritage.org/culture/.
8. Rachel Greszler and Romina Boccia, "Social Security Trustees Report: Unfunded Liability Increased $1.1 Trillion and Projected Insolvency in 2033," The Heritage Foundation, August 4, 2014, http://www.heritage.org/research/reports/2014

/08/social-security-trustees-report-unfunded-liability-increased-11-trillion-and
-projected-insolvency-in-2033; Robert E. Moffit and Alyene Senger, "The 2014
Medicare Trustees Report: A Dire Future for Seniors and Taxpayers without Reform,"
The Heritage Foundation, August 1, 2014, http://www.heritage.org/research/reports
/2014/08/the-2014-medicare-trustees-report-a-dire-future-for-seniors-and-taxpayers
-without-reform.

9. Marina Koren, "The Government Is Cracking Down on School Bake Sales," *National Journal*, July 25, 2014, http://www.nationaljournal.com/domesticpolicy/the-government
-is-cracking-down-on-school-bake-sales-20140725.

10. Lawrence M. Mead, *From Prophecy to Charity: How to Help the Poor* (Washington, DC: AEI Press, 2011), 31.

11. Franklin D. Roosevelt, "Annual Message to Congress" (speech, Washington, DC, January 4, 1935).

12. Ryan, *The Way Forward*, 140–42.

13. Robert Doar, "Ten Welfare-Reform Lessons," *National Review*, April 21, 2014, http://www.nationalreview.com/article/375679/ten-welfare-reform-lessons-robert-doar.

14. Mead, *From Prophecy to Charity*, 72–86.

15. Ron Haskins, "Getting Ahead in America," *National Affairs*, no. 1 (Fall 2009): 48, http://www.nationalaffairs.com/publications/detail/getting-ahead-in-america.

16. Mead, *From Prophecy to Charity*, 28–29.

TAXES AND SPENDING

1. Compañía General de Tabacos de Filipinas v. Collector of Internal Revenue, 275 U.S. 87, 100 (1927), http://caselaw.lp.findlaw.com/cgi-bin/getcase.pl?court=us&vol=275&invol=87.

2. Aristotle, *Politics*, Book 5, Chapter XI.

3. "Wasteful Spending List," Office of US Congressman Bill Posey, accessed August 29, 2014, http://posey.house.gov/wasteful-spending/.

4. The CCH Standard Federal Tax Reporter contained 73,954 pages for 2013.

5. Kyle Pomerleau and Lyman Stone, "Tax Freedom Day 2014 Is April 21, Three Days Later Than Last Year," Tax Foundation, April 7, 2014, http://taxfoundation.org/article/tax-freedom-day-2014-april-21-three-days-later-last-year.

6. Romina Boccia, "Federal Spending by the Numbers, 2014: Government Spending Trends in Graphics, Tables, and Key Points (Including 51 Examples of Government Waste)," The Heritage Foundation, December 8, 2014, http://www.heritage.org/research/reports/2014/12/federal-spending-by-the-numbers-2014.

7. Romina Boccia, "The Sure Path to American Decline," The Heritage Foundation, November 6, 2013, http://www.heritage.org/research/commentary/2013/11/the-sure-path-to-american-decline.

8. Kyle Pomerleau, "Tax Freedom Day 2015 Is April 24th," Tax Foundation, March 30, 2015, http://taxfoundation.org/article/tax-freedom-day-2015-april-24th.

9. Boccia, "Federal Spending by the Numbers, 2014."

10. Andrew Lundeen, "Do the Rich Pay Their Fair Share?" *Tax Foundation* (blog), April 17, 2014, http://taxfoundation.org/blog/do-rich-pay-their-fair-share.

11. See Luke 12:48.

12. Kyle Pomerleau, "Corporate Income Tax Rates around the World, 2014," *Tax Foundation* (blog), August 20, 2014, http://taxfoundation.org/article/corporate-income-tax-rates-around-world-2014.

13. Andrew Lundeen, "The Top 1 Percent Pays More in Taxes than the Bottom 90 Percent," *Tax Foundation* (blog), January 7, 2014, http://taxfoundation.org/blog /top-1-percent-pays-more-taxes-bottom-90-percent.

GOVERNMENT DEBT

1. Debt estimate figures from US Debt Clock.org, http://www.usdebtclock.org/ (accessed February 25, 2015).
2. Romina Boccia, "Federal Spending by the Numbers, 2014: Government Spending Trends in Graphics, Tables, and Key Points (Including 51 Examples of Government Waste)," The Heritage Foundation, December 8, 2014, http://www.heritage.org /research/reports/2014/12/federal-spending-by-the-numbers-2014.
3. Nicole Kaeding, "The Entitlement Spending Tsunami," *The Daily Caller*, August 27, 2014, http://dailycaller.com/2014/08/27/the-entitlement-spending-tsunami/.
4. Michael Tanner, "D.C. Forgets about the Debt," *National Review*, July 23, 2014, http://www.nationalreview.com/article/383425/dc-forgets-about-debt-michael -tanner.
5. Stephen Moore, "Don't Cry for Argentina—Cry for Us," The Heritage Foundation, August 6, 2014, http://www.heritage.org/research/commentary/2014/8/dont-cry-for -argentina-cry-for-us.
6. Nathan Bomey and John Gallagher, "How Detroit Went Broke: The Answers May Surprise You—And Don't Blame Coleman Young," *Detroit Free Press*, September 15, 2013, http://www.freep.com/interactive/article/20130915/NEWS01/130801004 /Detroit-Bankruptcy-history-1950-debt-pension-revenue.
7. Chris Good, "57 Terrible Consequences of the Sequester," ABC News, February 21, 2013, http://abcnews.go.com/Politics/OTUS/57-terrible-consequences-sequester /story?id=18551994.
8. Stephanie McNeal, "Despite Doomsday Predictions, Report Finds Only 1 Layoff from Sequester Cuts," FoxNews.com, May 8, 2014, http://www.foxnews.com/politics/2014 /05/07/despite-doomsday-predictions-sequester-cuts-only-led-to-1-layoff-in-2013/.

INDIVIDUAL LIBERTY

1. James Madison, "Speech at the Virginia Convention to Ratify the Federal Constitution" (Richmond, VA, June 6, 1788).
2. Bernie Becker, "Lerner: Talk Radio Listeners Are 'A—holes,'" *The Hill*, July 30, 2014, http://thehill.com/policy/finance/213792-new-emails-lerner-cursed-conservatives.
3. Caroline May, "Global Warming Activists Seek to Purge 'Deniers' among Local Weathermen," *Daily Caller*, January 30, 2012, http://dailycaller.com/2012/01/30 /global-warming-activists-seek-to-purge-deniers-among-local-weathermen/.
4. Michael Volpe, "Chick-fil-A Not Welcome in Chicago, Either," *Daily Caller*, July 26, 2012, http://dailycaller.com/2012/07/26/chick-fil-a-not-welcome-in-chicago-either/.
5. Isabel Knight, Martin Froger-Silva, and Eduard Saakashvili, "Students Share Mixed Responses to George/West Collection," *Daily Gazette*, February 13, 2014, http:// daily.swarthmore.edu/2014/02/13/students-share-mixed-responses-to-georgewest -collection/.
6. Associated Press, "Brandeis Withdraws Honorary Degree for Islam Critic Ayaan Hirsi Ali," April 9, 2014, http://www.theguardian.com/world/2014/apr/09/brandeis -withdraws-honorary-degree-ayaan-hirsi-ali-college.

7. Sandra Y. L. Korn, "The Doctrine of Academic Freedom: Let's Give Up on Academic Freedom in Favor of Justice," *Harvard Crimson*, February 18, 2014, http://www.the crimson.com/column/the-red-line/article/2014/2/18/academic-freedom-justice/.

8. Marc A. Thiessen, "Thanks to Jonathan Gruber for Revealing Obamacare Deception," *Washington Post*, November 17, 2014, http://www.washingtonpost.com/opinions/marc -thiessen-thanks-to-jonathan-gruber-for-revealing-obamacare-deception/2014/11/17 /356514b2-6e72-11e4-893f-86bd390a3340_story.html?hpid=z3.

9. See, for example, Mark Gius, "An Examination of the Effects of Concealed Weapons Laws and Assault Weapons Bans on State-Level Murder Rates," *Applied Economics Letters* 21, no. 4 (2014), published online November 26, 2013, http://www.tandf online.com/doi/abs/10.1080/13504851.2013.854294#.VEZ57OktCM_.

10. Mary Chastain, "ISIS: 'We Are the Soldiers of the Caliphate State and We Are Coming,'" Breitbart News, August 10, 2014, http://www.breitbart.com/Big-Peace /2014/08/10/ISIS-We-are-the-soldiers-of-the-Caliphate-state-and-we-are-Coming.

11. Todd Starnes, "Houston to Pastors: Forget Your Sermons, Now We Want Your Speeches," FoxNews.com, October 17, 2014, http://www.foxnews.com/opinion /2014/10/17/houston-to-pastors-forget-your-sermons-now-want-your-speeches/.

THE RULE OF LAW

1. Stephanie Condon, "IRS: Progressive Groups Flagged, but Tea Party Bigger Target," CBSNews.com, June 27, 2013, http://www.cbsnews.com/news/irs-progressive -groups-flagged-but-tea-party-bigger-target/; David Nather, Tarini Parti, and Byron Tau, "The IRS Wants YOU—To Share Everything," Politico, May 14, 2013, http:// www.politico.com/story/2013/05/the-irs-wants-you-to-share-everything-91378 .html.

2. "Camp Sends More Evidence of Criminal Wrongdoing to DOJ," US House Committee on Ways and Means, July 30, 2014, http://waysandmeans.house.gov /news/documentsingle.aspx?DocumentID=389786.

3. Barack Obama, interview by Bill O'Reilly, Fox News, February 2, 2014, http://video .foxnews.com/v/3142612336001/bill-oreillys-super-bowl-interview-with-president -obama/#sp=show-clips.

4. Abraham Lincoln, "Address before the Young Men's Lyceum of Springfield, Illinois" (January 27, 1838).

5. Joseph Postell, "From Administrative State to Constitutional Government," The Heritage Foundation, December 14, 2012, http://www.heritage.org/research /reports/2012/12/from-administrative-state-to-constitutional-government.

6. James Madison, "Federalist No. 47," in Alexander Hamilton, James Madison, and John Jay, *The Federalist Papers*, 1788.

7. Doe v. Bolton, 410 US 179 (1973).

8. Ronald Reagan, "Remarks at the Swearing-In Ceremony for Anthony M. Kennedy as an Associate Justice of the Supreme Court of the United States" (Washington, DC, February 18, 1988), http://www.presidency.ucsb.edu/ws/?pid=35439.

IMMIGRATION

1. Paul Ryan, *The Way Forward* (New York: Twelve, 2014), 201.

2. Ronald Reagan, "Thanksgiving Day Proclamation" (September 27, 1982).

3. Jessica Vaughan, "Catch and Release: Interior Immigration Enforcement in 2013," Center for Immigration Studies, March 2014, http://cis.org/catch-and-release.
4. Steven A. Camarota, "Welfare Use by Immigrant Households with Children: A Look at Cash, Medicaid, Housing, and Food Programs," Center for Immigration Studies, April 2011, http://cis.org/immigrant-welfare-use-2011.
5. Abraham Lincoln, "Speech at Chicago, Illinois" (July 10, 1858).
6. Paul Taylor, Mark Hugo Lopez, Jessica Martínez, and Gabriel Velasco, "When Labels Don't Fit: Hispanics and Their Views of Identity," Pew Research Center, April 4, 2012, http://www.pewhispanic.org/2012/04/04/when-labels-dont-fit-hispanics-and-their-views-of-identity/.

MARIJUANA
1. Lydia Saad, "Majority Continues to Support Pot Legalization in U.S.," Gallup, November 6, 2014, http://www.gallup.com/poll/179195/majority-continues-support-pot-legalization.aspx.
2. William J. Bennett and Robert A. White, *Going to Pot* (New York: Center Street, 2015), xiv.
3. Ibid., 15–16.
4. Ibid., 20–21.
5. Ibid., 6.
6. Ibid., 12–13.
7. Ibid., 28.
8. Ibid., 27.
9. Ibid., 26.
10. Ibid., 139.
11. Ibid., 147.
12. Ibid., 170.
13. Ibid., 25.
14. Ibid., 153–54.
15. Ibid., 77–79.
16. Ibid., 72–77, 101–102, 174–75.
17. Ibid., xix.
18. Ibid., 54.
19. Ibid., 53.
20. Ibid., 61.
21. Ibid., 49.
22. Ibid., xvii.
23. Ibid., 35.
24. Ibid., 112.
25. Ibid., 9.
26. William J. Bennett, *The De-valuing of America* (New York: Summit Books, 1992), 120.

RACE, CLASS, GENDER, AND ETHNICITY
1. Jake Tapper, "VP Biden Says Republicans Are 'Going to Put Y'all Back in Chains,'" *ABC News Political Punch* (blog), August 14, 2012, http://abcnews.go.com/blogs/politics/2012/08/vp-biden-says-republicans-are-going-to-put-yall-back-in-chains/.

2. Brendan Bordelon, "Charlie Rangel: Some in GOP 'Believe That Slavery Isn't Over,'" *National Review*, October 31, 2014, http://www.nationalreview.com/corner/391585/charlie-rangel-some-gop-believe-slavery-isnt-over-brendan-bordelon.

3. John McCormack, "Harry Reid: 'I Don't Know How Anyone of Hispanic Heritage Could Be a Republican,'" *The Weekly Standard* (blog), August 10, 2010, http://www.weeklystandard.com/blogs/harry-reid-i-dont-know-how-anyone-hispanic-heritage-could-be-republican.

4. Stanley B. Greenberg et al., "The Very Separate World of Conservative Republicans" Democracy Corps, October 16, 2009, http://www.democracycorps.com/News/the-very-separate-world-of-conservative-republicans/.

5. Condoleezza Rice, interview on *Fox and Friends*, Fox News, November 6, 2014, http://video.foxnews.com/v/3878300052001/condoleeza-rices-take-on-americas-political-landscape/.

6. Barack Obama, "Full Transcript: Sen. Barack Obama's Victory Speech," ABC News, November 4, 2008, http://abcnews.go.com/Politics/Vote2008/story?id=6181477.

7. Walt Whitman, preface to *Leaves of Grass*.

8. Michael Moore, interview by Piers Morgan, *Piers Morgan Tonight*, CNN, September 26, 2011, http://transcripts.cnn.com/TRANSCRIPTS/1109/26/pmt.01.html.

9. James Piereson, "The Truth about the 'One Percent,'" *Wall Street Journal*, February 18, 2014, http://www.manhattan-institute.org/html/miarticle.htm?id=10062#.VF0tGOktCM8.

10. Mark R. Rank, "From Rags to Riches to Rags," *New York Times*, April 18, 2014, http://www.nytimes.com/2014/04/20/opinion/sunday/from-rags-to-riches-to-rags.html?smid=pl-share&_r=0.

11. Viktor E. Frankl, *Man's Search for Meaning*, 4th ed. (Boston: Beacon Press, 1992), 94.

NATIONAL DEFENSE

1. Daniel Webster, "Remarks in the US Senate" (Washington, DC, June 3, 1834).

2. John Jay, "Federalist No. 3," in Alexander Hamilton, James Madison, and John Jay, *The Federalist Papers* (1788).

3. George Washington, "First Annual Message to Congress on the State of the Union," (New York, January 8, 1790).

4. Ronald Reagan, "Address Accepting the Presidential Nomination at the Republican National Convention in Detroit" (July 17, 1980).

5. Vaclav Havel, Jose María Aznar, Jose-Manuel Durão Barroso, Silvio Berlusconi, Tony Blair, Peter Medgyessy, Leszek Miller, and Anders Fogh Rasmussen, "United We Stand: Eight European Leaders Are As One with President Bush," *Wall Street Journal*, January 30, 2003, http://www.aei.org/publication/united-we-stand/.

6. Amy Belasco, *The Cost of Iraq, Afghanistan, and Other Global War on Terror Operations since 9/11* (US Library of Congress, Congressional Research Service, Report RL33110, December 8, 2014), https://www.fas.org/sgp/crs/natsec/RL33110.pdf.

7. Romina Boccia, "Federal Spending by the Numbers, 2014: Government Spending Trends in Graphics, Tables, and Key Points (Including 51 Examples of Government Waste)," The Heritage Foundation, December 8, 2014, http://www.heritage.org/research/reports/2014/12/federal-spending-by-the-numbers-2014.

8. Ernesto Londoño, "Pentagon Blueprint Would Cut Army Size as Military Adjusts to Leaner Budgets," *Washington Post*, February 24, 2014, http://www.washingtonpost

.com/world/national-security/pentagon-blueprint-would-cut-army-size-as-military
-adjusts-to-leaner-budgets/2014/02/24/c029e2b4-9d8d-11e3-9ba6-800d1192d08b
_story.html.

9. Guo Renjie, ed., "DM Spokesman: China-Russia Military Cooperation Shows High-Level Mutual Trust," Chinese Ministry of National Defense, May 29, 2014, http://eng.mod.gov.cn/Press/2014-05/29/content_4512828.htm.

10. David D. Lee, *Sergeant York: An American Hero* (Lexington: University Press of Kentucky, 1985), 109.

ISLAMIC TERRORISM

1. Christine Rousselle, "Leader of Islamic State Claims Rome Will Be Conquered Next," Townhall.com, July 2, 2014, http://townhall.com/tipsheet/christinerousselle/2014/07/02/leader-of-islamic-state-claims-rome-will-be-conquered-next-n1858160.

2. Salma Abdelaziz, "Death and Desecration in Syria: Jihadist Group 'Crucifies' Bodies to Send Message," CNN, May 2, 2014, http://www.cnn.com/2014/05/01/world/meast/syria-bodies-crucifixions/.

3. Maria Abi-Habib, "The Child Soldiers Who Escaped Islamic State," *Wall Street Journal*, December 26, 2014, http://www.wsj.com/articles/the-child-soldiers-who-escaped-islamic-state-1419628277.

4. "Full Text of the Last E-mail the Islamic State Sent to the Foley Family," *GlobalPost*, August 21, 2014, http://www.globalpost.com/dispatch/news/regions/middle-east/syria/140821/text-last-email-islamic-state-sent-foley-family.

5. "The World's Muslims: Religion, Politics and Society," Pew Research Center, April 30, 2013, http://www.pewforum.org/2013/04/30/the-worlds-muslims-religion-politics-society-overview/.

6. Bernard Lewis, "License to Kill: Usama bin Ladin's Declaration of Jihad," *Foreign Affairs* (November/December 1998), http://www.foreignaffairs.com/articles/54594/bernard-lewis/license-to-kill-usama-bin-ladins-declaration-of-jihad.

7. William J. Bennett and Seth Leibsohn, *The Fight of Our Lives* (Nashville: Thomas Nelson, 2011), xii.

8. Freedom House's *Freedom in the World 2014*, a country report on Iran, is available at https://freedomhouse.org/report/freedom-world/2014/iran#.VQrzYulFCM8.

9. Matthias Küntzel, "Ahmadinejad's Demons," *New Republic*, April 24, 2006, http://www.matthiaskuentzel.de/contents/ahmadinejads-demons.

10. Reza Kahlili, "Iran's Supreme Leader: Jihad Will Continue until America Is No More," *Daily Caller*, May 25, 2014, http://dailycaller.com/2014/05/25/irans-supreme-leader-jihad-will-continue-until-america-is-no-more/.

11. Sheik Ibrahim Madhi, sermon broadcast by Palestinian Authority television, June 8, 2001, in "Palestinian Incitement against Jews and Israel Continues in Mosque Sermon," Anti-Defamation League archive, http://archive.adl.org/israel/mosque_sermon2.html.

12. Mark Suppelsa, "Photo Implies ISIS Threat to Chicago," WGNtv.com, August 21, 2014, http://wgntv.com/2014/08/21/photo-implies-isis-threat-to-chicago/.

13. Jamie Weinstein, "ISIS Threatens America: 'We Will Raise the Flag of Allah in the White House,'" *Daily Caller*, August 8, 2014, http://dailycaller.com/2014/08/08/isis-threatens-america-we-will-raise-the-flag-of-allah-in-the-white-house/.

14. Bernard Lewis, *Faith and Power* (New York: Oxford University Press, 2010), 166.
15. Adam Housley, "Sources: US Letting Benghazi Suspects off Hook, Recent Arrest 'Small Potatoes,'" FoxNews.com, June 27, 2014, http://www.foxnews.com/politics /2014/06/27/sources-us-letting-benghazi-suspects-off-hook-recent-arrest-small -potatoes/.

TRADITIONAL VALUES

1. Russell Kirk, "Ten Conservative Principles" (lecture, The Heritage Foundation, Washington, DC, March 20, 1986), http://www.heritage.org/initiatives/first -principles/primary-sources/the-ten-conservative-principles-of-russell-kirk.
2. Joseph Conrad, *The Nigger of the 'Narcissus': A Tale of the Forecastle* (1897), chapter 1.
3. Aristotle, *Politics*, book 3, part IV.
4. Abraham Lincoln, "Peoria Speech," (Peoria, IL, October 16, 1854).
5. Caleb Bonham, "VIDEO: Harvard Students Claim America Is a Bigger Threat to Peace than ISIS," Campus Reform, October 7, 2014, http://www.campusreform.org /?ID=5962.
6. Abraham Lincoln, "First Inaugural Address" (Washington, DC, March 4, 1861).
7. Livy, *The History of Rome*, preface.
8. Tacitus, *Annals*, 3.65.

MARRIAGE AND FAMILY

1. "Marriage Rates Hit New, All-Time Low," WTTG Fox 5 News, October 14, 2014, http://www.myfoxdc.com/story/26779009/marriage-rates-hit-new-all-time-low.
2. Ron Haskins, "Marriage, Parenthood, and Public Policy," *National Affairs*, no. 19 (Spring 2014), http://www.nationalaffairs.com/publications/detail/marriage -parenthood-and-public-policy.
3. Joyce A. Martin et al., "Births: Final Data for 2012," *National Vital Statistics Reports*, vol. 62, no. 9, National Center for Health Statistics, December 30, 2013, p. 7, Table C, http://www.cdc.gov/nchs/fastats/unmarried-childbearing.htm.
4. Haskins, "Marriage, Parenthood, and Public Policy."
5. William J. Bennett, *The Broken Hearth* (New York: Doubleday, 2001), 18–19.
6. Haskins, "Marriage, Parenthood, and Public Policy."
7. Christine Kim, "Academic Success Begins at Home: How Children Can Succeed in School," The Heritage Foundation, September 22, 2008, http://www.heritage .org/research/reports/2008/09/academic-success-begins-at-home-how-children-can -succeed-in-school.
8. Aristotle, *Politics*, Book I, Part II.
9. Haskins, "Marriage, Parenthood, and Public Policy."
10. Robert Maranto and Michael Crouch, "Ignoring an Inequality Culprit: Single-Parent Families," *Wall Street Journal*, April 20, 2014, http://online.wsj.com/news/articles/SB 10001424052702303603904579493612156024266.
11. Haskins, "Marriage, Parenthood, and Public Policy"; "Why Fathers Matter," FamilyFacts.org, http://www.familyfacts.org/briefs/25/why-fathers-matter; "More than Breadwinners: The Myriad Ways in Which Fathers Contribute to Family Well-Being," FamilyFacts.org, June 14, 2013, http://www.familyfacts.org/briefs/45/more-than -breadwinners-the-myriad-ways-in-which-fathers-contribute-to-family-well-being.

12. Elayne Bennett, *Daughters in Danger: Helping Our Girls Thrive in Today's Culture* (Nashville: Thomas Nelson, 2014), 127–28; Meg Meeker, *Strong Fathers, Strong Daughters: 10 Secrets Every Father Should Know* (New York: Ballantine Books, 2007), 23–24.
13. "The Benefits of Marriage," FamilyFacts.org, http://www.familyfacts.org/briefs/1/the -benefits-of-marriage.
14. Theodore Roosevelt, *Theodore Roosevelt: An Autobiography*, chapter 9.
15. George Eliot, *Adam Bede*, chapter 54.
16. The Sacrament of Matrimony, *Catechism of the Catholic Church*, 2nd ed. (1997), part 2, sec. 2, ch. 3, article 7.
17. Justin McCarthy, "Same-Sex Marriage Support Reaches New High at 55%," Gallup, May 21, 2014, http://www.gallup.com/poll/169640/sex-marriage-support-reaches -new-high.aspx.
18. Ibid.

FAITH AND RELIGION

1. 2 Corinthians 3:17, NLT.
2. Michael Novak, *On Two Wings: Humble Faith and Common Sense at the American Founding* (San Francisco: Encounter Books, 2002), 13.
3. William J. Bennett, *Our Sacred Honor: Words of Advice from the Founders in Stories, Letters, Poems, and Speeches* (New York: Simon & Schuster, 1997), 381.
4. Novak, *On Two Wings*, 6.
5. John F. Kennedy, "Inaugural Address," (Washington, DC, January 20, 1961).
6. Bennett, *Our Sacred Honor*, 365.
7. Ibid., 370.
8. Novak, *On Two Wings*, 58.
9. Todd Starnes, "Lawsuit Filed: Jesus Not Welcome in Nazareth, Pa. School," Todd's American Dispatch, April 10, 2014, http://www.foxnews.com/opinion/2014/04/10 /lawsuit-filed-jesus-not-welcome-in-nazareth-pa-school/.
10. "Maryland School District to Strip References to Religious Holidays on School Calendars," FoxNews.com, November 12, 2014, http://www.foxnews.com/us/2014 /11/12/maryland-school-district-to-strip-references-to-religious-holidays-on-school/.
11. Todd Starnes, "University Removes 'God' from Plaque," Todd's American Dispatch, February 27, 2014, http://www.foxnews.com/opinion/2014/02/27/purdue-university -removes-god-from-plaque/.
12. Todd Starnes, "Bibles Removed from University of Wisconsin Lodge," Todd's American Dispatch, January 24, 2014, http://www.foxnews.com/opinion/2014/01/24/bibles -removed-from-university-lodge/.
13. "Global Religious Diversity," Pew Research Center's Religion and Public Life Project, April 4, 2014, http://www.pewforum.org/2014/04/04/global-religious-diversity/.
14. Frank Newport, "More Than 9 in 10 Americans Continue to Believe in God," Gallup, June 3, 2011, http://www.gallup.com/poll/147887/americans-continue-believe-god.aspx.
15. Michael Lipka, "What Surveys Say about Worship Attendance—and Why Some Stay Home," Pew Research Center, September 13, 2013, http://www.pewresearch.org /fact-tank/2013/09/13/what-surveys-say-about-worship-attendance-and-why-some -stay-home/.

16. "'Nones' on the Rise," Pew Research Center's Religion and Public Life Project, October 9, 2012, http://www.pewforum.org/2012/10/09/nones-on-the-rise/.

17. "Giving USA: Americans Gave $335.17 Billion to Charity in 2013," Lilly Family School of Philanthropy, Indiana University–Purdue University Indianapolis, June 17, 2014, http://www.philanthropy.iupui.edu/news/article/giving-usa-2014.

18. "Reducing Teens' Risk and the Role of Religiosity," FamilyFacts.org, available at http://www.familyfacts.org/briefs/29/reducing-teens-risk-and-the-role-of-religiosity.

19. Bennett, *Our Sacred Honor*, 381–82.

ABORTION

1. "Abortion: Some Medical Facts," National Right to Life, http://www.nrlc.org/abortion/medicalfacts/techniques/; Randall K. O'Bannon, "There Is No Such Thing As a 'Humane' Late Abortion," National Right to Life News Today, August 23, 2013, http://www.nationalrighttolifenews.org/news/2013/08/there-is-no-such-thing-as-a-humane-late-abortion/#.VN1kquk5CM-.

2. Peter Wehner, "The Nasty, Brutish World of Richard Dawkins," *Commentary*, August 21, 2014, http://www.commentarymagazine.com/2014/08/21/the-nasty-brutish-world-of-richard-dawkins/.

3. Guy Benson, "CNN Poll: 58 Percent of Americans Oppose Abortion in All or Most Cases," Townhall.com, March 10, 2014, http://townhall.com/tipsheet/guybenson/2014/03/10/cnn-poll-58-percent-of-americans-oppose-abortion-in-all-or-most-circumstances-n1806283.

4. Doe v. Bolton, 410 US 179 (1973).

5. Cathy Cleaver Ruse and Rob Schwarzwalder, "The Best Pro-Life Arguments for Secular Audiences," Family Research Council, http://www.frc.org/brochure/the-best-pro-life-arguments-for-secular-audiences.

6. "Abortion Statistics: United States Data and Trends," National Right to Life Committee, February 2014, http://www.nrlc.org/communications/abortionnumbers/.

7. "Summary of Known Health-Risks of Abortion," Americans United for Life, 2013, http://www.aul.org/wp-content/uploads/2013/08/Summary-of-Known-Health-Risks-of-Abortion.pdf.

8. Ruse and Schwarzwalder, "The Best Pro-Life Arguments."

9. "Your Growing Belly and Baby: A Timeline through Pregnancy," WebMD, accessed February 20, 2015, http://www.webmd.com/baby/interactive-pregnancy-tool-fetal-development.

10. Arina Grossu, "What Science Reveals about Fetal Pain," Family Research Council, January 2015, http://frc.org/fetalpain.

11. "Newborn Loss: Neonatal Death," March of Dimes Foundation, January 2010, http://www.marchofdimes.org/loss/neonatal-death.aspx.

12. William L. Saunders Jr., Cathy Cleaver Ruse, and Lucia Papayova, "The Top Ten Myths about Abortion," Family Research Council, 2007, http://www.frc.org/get.cfm?i=BC07J02.

13. Martha Shuping and Christopher Gacek, "Post-Abortion Suffering: A Psychiatrist Looks at the Effects of Abortion," Family Research Council, 2010, http://downloads.frc.org/EF/EF10B09.pdf.

14. Rachel Cooke, "Gloria Steinem: 'I Think We Need to Get Much Angrier,'" *Observer*, November 12, 2011, http://www.theguardian.com/books/2011/nov/13/gloria-steinem -interview-feminism-abortion?newsfeed=true.
15. Testimonies from the Silent No More Awareness Campaign, accessed September 28, 2014, http://www.silentnomoreawareness.org/.

K–12 EDUCATION

1. Thomas Jefferson, letter to George Wythe, August 13, 1786.
2. Thomas Jefferson, et al., "Report of the Commissioners Appointed to Fix the Site of the University of Virginia," August 4, 1818.
3. Mary Beth Marklein, "SAT, ACT: Most High School Kids Lack Skills for College," *USA Today*, September 25, 2012, http://usatoday30.usatoday.com/news/nation/story /2012/09/24/sat-act-most-high-school-kids-lack-skills-for-college/57836602/1.
4. "2013 Mathematics and Reading: Grade 12 Assessments," National Assessment of Educational Progress (NAEP), http://www.nationsreportcard.gov/reading_math _g12_2013/#/.
5. Lyndsey Layton, "U.S. Students Lag around Average on International Science, Math and Reading Test," *Washington Post*, December 3, 2013, http://www.washingtonpost .com/local/education/us-students-lag-around-average-on-international-science-math -and-reading-test/2013/12/02/2e510f26-5b92-11e3-a49b-90a0e156254b_story.html.
6. Masuma Ahuja, "Teens Are Spending More Time Consuming Media, on Mobile Devices," *Washington Post*, March 13, 2013, http://www.washingtonpost.com/postlive /teens-are-spending-more-time-consuming-media-on-mobile-devices/2013/03/12 /309bb242-8689-11e2-98a3-b3db6b9ac586_story.html.
7. Allie Bidwell, "Students Spend More Time on Homework but Teachers Say It's Worth It," *U.S. News & World Report*, February 27, 2014, http://www.usnews.com /news/articles/2014/02/27/students-spend-more-time-on-homework-but-teachers -say-its-worth-it.
8. "Total and Current Expenditures per Pupil in Public Elementary and Secondary Schools: Selected Years, 1919–20 through 2010–11," *Digest of Education Statistics*, US Department of Education, accessed September 15, 2014, http://nces.ed.gov /programs/digest/d13/tables/dt13_236.55.asp.
9. Associated Press, "U.S. Education Spending Tops Global List, Study Shows," June 25, 2013, http://www.cbsnews.com/news/us-education-spending-tops-global-list-study -shows/.
10. "The Federal Role in Education," US Department of Education, last modified February 13, 2012, http://www2.ed.gov/about/overview/fed/role.html.
11. Lisa Snell, "Educational Achievement," *2014 Index of Culture and Opportunity*, ed. Jennifer A. Marshall and Rea S. Hederman Jr. (The Heritage Foundation, 2014), 61–62, http://index.heritage.org/culture/; Andrew J. Coulson, "School Funding System Not Broken . . . It Just Doesn't Work," *Cato at Liberty* (blog), Cato Institute, May 7, 2013, http://www.cato.org/blog/school-funding-system-not-broken-it-just -doesnt-work.
12. Martin Luther King Jr., "The Purpose of Education," *The Maroon Tiger*, Morehouse College, Jan–Feb 1947, http://mlk-kpp01.stanford.edu/index.php/encyclopedia /documentsentry/doc_470200_000/.

13. "The Nation's Report Card: U.S. History 2010," National Center for Education Statistics, 2011, 37, http://nces.ed.gov/nationsreportcard/pubs/main2010/2011468.asp.

14. "Americans Know Surprisingly Little about Their Government, Survey Finds," The Annenberg Public Policy Center, September 17, 2014, http://www.annenberg publicpolicycenter.org/americans-know-surprisingly-little-about-their-government -survey-finds/.

HIGHER EDUCATION

1. William J. Bennett and David Wilezol, *Is College Worth It?* (Nashville: Thomas Nelson, 2013), 152–54.

2. Kevin Eagan et al., "Undergraduate Teaching Faculty: The 2013–2014 HERI Faculty Survey," Higher Education Research Institute, University of California, Los Angeles (2014), 39, http://www.heri.ucla.edu/facPublications.php.

3. Sita Slavov, "Surviving Academe's Liberal Bias," *Chronicle of Higher Education*, October 3, 2012, http://chronicle.com/blogs/conversation/2012/10/03/surviving -academes-liberal-bias/.

4. Bennett and Wilezol, *Is College Worth It?*, 153.

5. Ryan Struyk, "What It's Like to Be a Conservative on a Liberal College Campus," ABC News, April 25, 2014, http://abcnews.go.com/Politics/conservative-liberal -college-campus/story?id=23443117.

6. Struyk, "Conservative on a Liberal College Campus."

7. "2014 Annual Commencement Speaker Survey," Young America's Foundation, May 19, 2014, http://www.yaf.org/2014YAFAnnualCommencementSpeakerSurvey.aspx.

8. Andrew Johnson, "Professor: 'Colleges Will Start Closing Up' If 'Racist, Misogynist, Money-Grubbing' GOP Wins," *National Review*, April 22, 2014, http://www.national review.com/corner/376331/professor-colleges-will-start-closing-if-racist-misogynist -money-grubbing-gop-wins.

9. Kate Edwards, "*The Daily Caller*: Outlandish College Courses: The Dirty Dozen for Private (non-Ivy League) Schools," Young America's Foundation, January 16, 2013, http://www.yaf.org/private-school-dirty-dozen.aspx; Kate Edwards, "*The Daily Caller* Opinion: Outlandish College Courses: The Public School Dirty Dozen," Young America's Foundation, January 17, 2013, http://www.yaf.org/public-school-dirty -dozen.aspx.

10. "A Crisis of Competence: The Corrupting Effect of Political Activism in the University of California," National Association of Scholars, April 2012, 37–38, http://www.nas.org /images/documents/A_Crisis_of_Competence.pdf.

11. "What Will They Learn? 2009: A Report on General Education Requirements at 100 of the Nation's Leading Colleges and Universities," American Council of Trustees and Alumni (2009), 3, http://www.goacta.org/publications/what_will_they_learn_2009; Leslie Ford, "The Lady Gaga-fication of Higher Ed," *The Daily Signal*, December 9, 2011, http://dailysignal.com/2011/12/09/the-lady-gaga-fication-of-higher-ed/.

12. Bennett and Wilezol, *Is College Worth It?*, 149–52.

13. Ibid., 131–34.

14. "A Crisis of Competence," 60.

15. "Fact Sheet: Summary of Findings from Survey of Hiring Decision-Makers," Accrediting Council for Independent Colleges and Schools (ACICS), November 2011, http://www .acics.org/events/content.aspx?id=4718.

16. Ramesh Ponnuru and Yuval Levin, "How Republicans Can Improve Higher Education," *Washington Post*, November 6, 2014, http://www.washingtonpost.com/opinions/how -republicans-can-improve-higher-education-and-help-the-party/2014/11/06/d82aeb02 -6532-11e4-836c-83bc4f26eb67_story.html.

17. Phil Izzo, "Congratulations to Class of 2014, Most Indebted Ever," *The Numbers* (blog), *Wall Street Journal*, May 16, 2014, http://blogs.wsj.com/numbers/congatulations -to-class-of-2014-the-most-indebted-ever-1368/.